Cabinets of Curiosities

Thames & Hudson

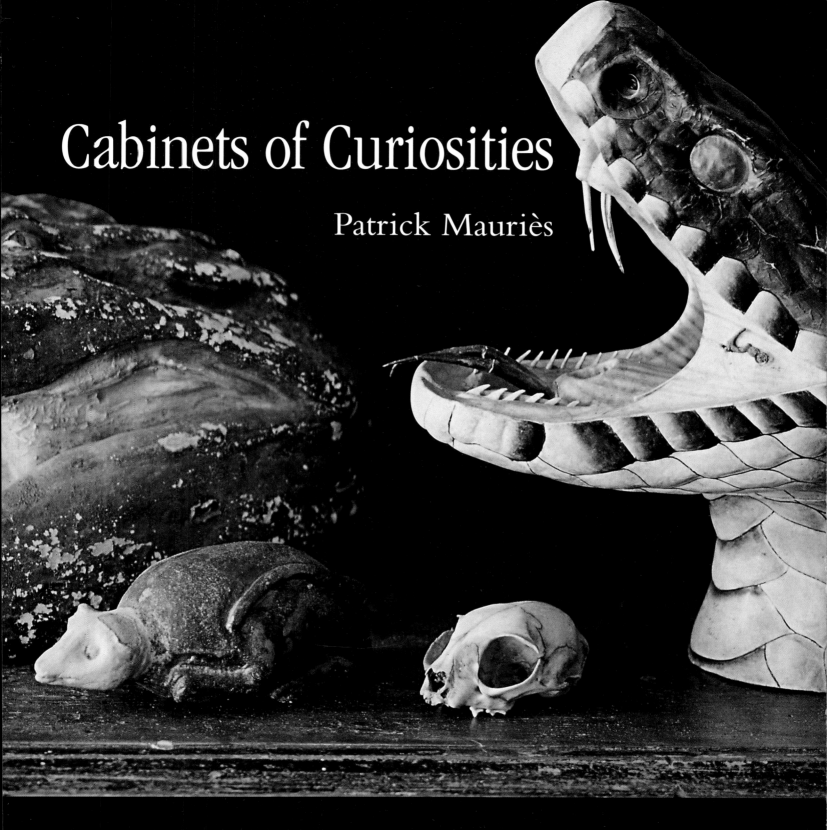

Cabinets of Curiosities

Patrick Mauriès

WITH 272 ILLUSTRATIONS, 139 IN COLOUR AND 133 IN DUOTONE

Endpapers Wunderkammer by Erik Desmazières, reproduced by kind permission of the artist

Half-title Trompe-l'oeil painting of a cabinet, 17th century, attributed to Domenico Remps

Title page from the collection of Françoise de Nobèle, Paris

This page Above Ostrich made from a misshapen pearl. Florentine, early 18th century. *Right* Cup made about 1560 in Antwerp; silver-gilt and painted nautilus shell.

Picture Research: Georgina Bruckner

First published in the United Kingdom in 2002 by
Thames & Hudson Ltd
181A High Holborn
London WC1V 7QX

www.thamesandhudson.com

British Library Cataloguing-in-Publication Data
A catalogue record for this book is available
from the British Library

ISBN 0-500-51091-1

Printed and bound in Italy by Conti Tipocolor

Prelude

The story of cabinets of curiosities is above all that of a handful of figures scattered throughout the length and breadth of Europe in the age of the Baroque. John Tradescant and Elias Ashmole in Oxford, Ulisse Aldrovandi and Manfredo Settala in Milan, Lodovico Moscardo in Verona, Ferdinando Cospi in Bologna, Père Molinet in Paris, Nicolas Pereisc in Aix-en-Provence, Olaeus Worms in Copenhagen, Leonhard Fuchs and Conrad Gessner in Basle and Zurich and one or two others, each in turn emerging from the arcane recesses of history to form a shadowy procession, wreathed in mists and attended a by a deluge of miscellaneous objects.

Several of their number have left us their portraits, proudly positioned as the frontispieces to their catalogues, but these images are more effigies than likenesses of living features: they conceal more than they reveal, offering only clumsy approximations of the idiosyncrasies of the flesh, or of quirks or eccentricities of expression now lost for ever.

It is hardly a matter of controversy to suggest that the majority of these enlightened collectors preferred the immutable and unmoving nature of objects to the illusions of a world in a constant state of flux and the turbulence of human passions. And it is this predilection for things devoid of life that – paradoxically – now brings them back to life again for us, and in far more vivid fashion than any portrait, however convincing. Amid the eclectic profusion of objects that they have bequeathed to us we may still discern their visions and desires; we can still touch with our own fingers the objects – scarcely any dustier now than then – that they once held, and we too can take pleasure in the symmetries and the variations in shape and colour that they coveted, classified, added to and modified with such obsessive devotion, day after day and year after year.

Oppressed by the cares of the world and by the fleeting nature of things and of the laws that govern them, these exceptional characters were possessed by an unattainable desire for perfect completeness, and united by a dogged and undeviating determination to compress the contents of an entire library into a single volume. And in the end they have indeed succeeded in defying time, setting against it a version of reality that is as incongruous as it is enduring.

The precursors of cabinets of curiosities can be found in the relic collections of medieval churches. The motive for possessing these relics was their supposed sanctity and the powers attributed to them to cure sickness. At first they consisted of things associated with Christ and his disciples, pieces of the True Cross, fragments of apostles' bones, etc. Soon the skeletons of saints were given equal veneration and as time went on the objects became increasingly bizarre – a vial of the Virgin's milk or Moses' rod – often enshrined in precious reliquaries. The abbey of St-Denis, near Paris, had one of the largest collections in Europe (left). Something of the atmosphere of the supernatural that belonged to them passed to cabinets of curiosities, so that alchemy, the occult and magic were never very far away.

'The Sense of Sight', by 'Velvet' Brueghel and Peter Paul Rubens, one of a series of 'The Five Senses' commissioned in 1617 by Albert and Isabella, governors of the Netherlands. The Archduke Albert was Rudolf II's brother and his wife Isabella the daughter of Philip II of Spain. Their collection of curiosities has been dispersed, but the paintings remain in the Prado, Madrid. The great allegorical canvases are a sort of pictorial equivalent of the cabinets, representing the same desire to bring all knowledge into a single space, and many indeed include items that they actually owned. 'The Sense of Sight' combines *naturalia* (shells, bottom right), scientific instruments (globe, armillary sphere, compasses, telescopes), coins, jewels, antiquities (Roman busts on the shelves behind) and works of art.

CURIOSITIES ON DISPLAY

The museum of Ferrante Imperato in Naples, the frontispiece of his catalogue, *Dell'historia naturale* (1599). Books, botanical and zoological specimens and jars are crowded together in carefully arranged profusion. Shells and marine creatures, including an enormous stuffed crocodile, are suspended from the ceiling. Imperato was an apothecary and used his collection for research and the manufacture of medicines. This is the earliest representation of a cabinet of curiosities. A guide, possibly Imperato himself, points out particular items to visitors. John Evelyn visited this museum in February 1645, 'one of the most observable palaces in the citty, the repository of incomparable rarities. Amongst the naturall herbals most remarkable was the Byssus marina and Pinna marina; the male and female cameleon; an Onacratulus; an extraordinary greate crocodile; some of the Orcades Anates, held here for a great rarity; likewise a salamander; the male and female Manucodiata, the male having an hollow in the back, in wch it is reported the female both layes and hatches her egg.'

BELOW Woodcut from Imperato's *Dell'historia naturale*.

OPPOSITE The 16th-century *studiolo* of Francesco I, Grand-duke of Tuscany. This tiny, windowless room in the Palazzo Vecchio, Florence, reflects the later Medici's preoccupation with art and the occult. The subject-matter of the paintings has much in common with a cabinet of curiosities: minerals (several pictures of mines), alchemy (a particular interest of Francesco I), nature (whale-fishing) and chemistry (gunpowder), as well as classical mythology. The upper paintings are on slate, the lower ones the doors of cupboards.

BELOW Frontispiece of Bacon's *Instauratia Magna.*

BACKGROUND Gilt bronze dolphin from the Medici collection, 16th-century.

In 1620, Francis Bacon selected as the frontispiece of his *Instauratio Magna,*[1] in which he proposed a wide-ranging revision of contemporary scholarship, the now-famous image of a ship in full sail upon a boundless sea. All that flanks this scene is a pair of columns: the Pillars of Hercules, marking the furthest reaches of the known world and the frontier of the unknown – the threshold of an enthralling, tantalising world of uncharted places and infinite spaces, as yet undiscovered and waiting only to be revealed to the human spirit.

At first sight it may seem contrary to open this brief history of cabinets of curiosities, the very essence of restricted, circumscribed collections, with the image of a ship setting out to sea. But in a number of ways, Bacon's metaphor succeeds in drawing together the scattered threads of the story of the cult of 'curiosities'; that is, the knowledge of liminal objects that lay on the margins of charted territory, brought back from worlds unknown, defying any accepted system of classification (and most notably the conventional categories of 'arts' and 'sciences'), and associated with the discovery of 'new worlds'. The jealously guarded privacy of the cabinet of curiosities has meaning only in relation to an absolute 'elsewhere', and to the things that are brought back from it. This outer realm, this elsewhere, is a source of wonders.

The twin pillars that mark the frontiers of the known world also provide a frame for the unknown. Similarly, the cabinet of curiosities finds its *raison d'être* in a multiplicity of frames, niches, boxes, drawers and cases, in appropriating to itself the chaos of the world and imposing upon it systems – however arbitrary – of symmetries and hierarchies. It is like a shadow cast by the 'unknown', an unknown that dissolves into a shower of objects. It offers an inexhaustible supply of fragments and relics painstakingly slotted and fitted into the elected space, heavy with meaning, of a secret room.

Engraving, frontispiece: here we find ourselves face to face with an image (and only an image) of the world. This same image, but this time in the form of maps, globes, *mappamundi* and armillary spheres, forms another favoured theme of cabinets of curiosities, offering a type of reduction that represents the ultimate in scaling down. For, once the false pretexts of scientific investigation and a quest for knowledge have been demolished, what other justification can there be for cabinets of curiosities except to conjure up images of the world, a miniature universe of textures, colours, materials and a multiplicity of forms?

The Cabinet of Francesco
Calzolari, from his *Museum
Calceolarium*, published in
Verona, 1622. Animals, birds
and fishes hang from the ceiling.
The shelves and drawers are also
crowded with natural and man-
made objects, while particularly
choice specimens are displayed
in a sort of altar at the end of the
room. Like Imperato, Calzolari
too was an apothecary.

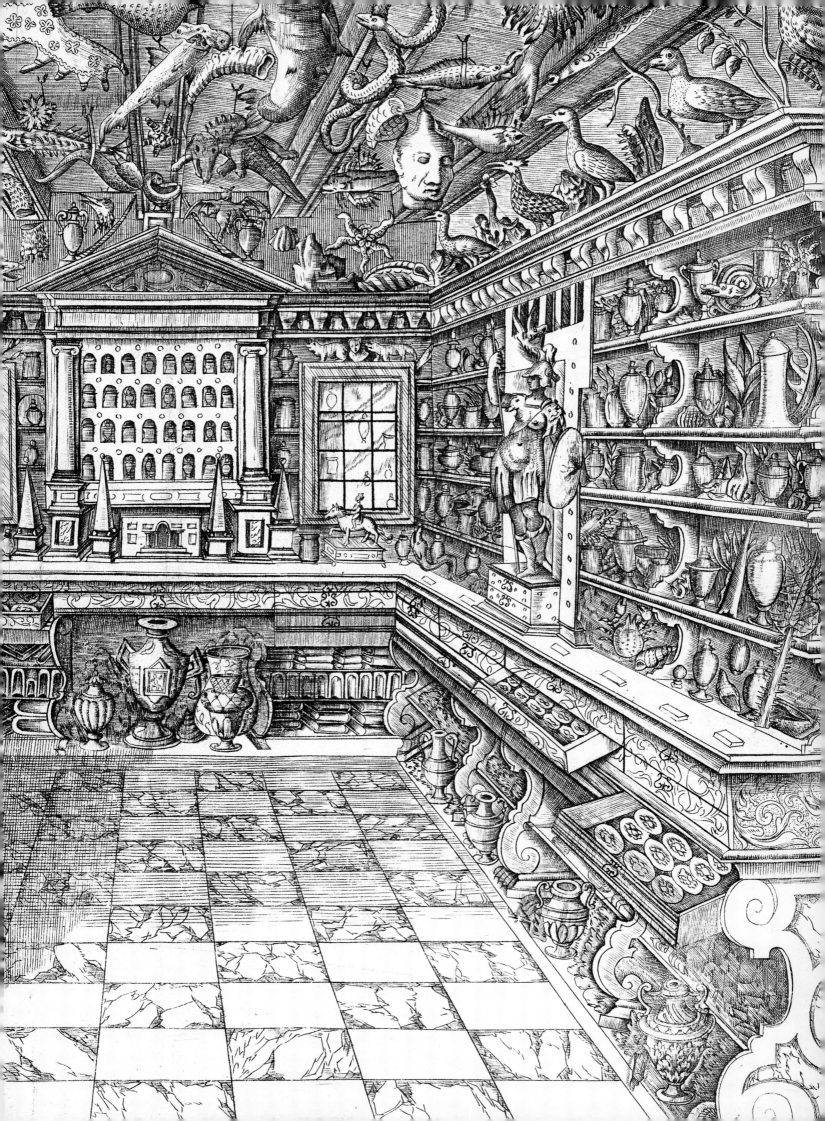

LEFT The Cabinet of Johann Septimus Jörger, mid-17th century. Jörger was a Protestant refugee from Austria who settled in Nuremberg. His collection was typical of the fairly wealthy connoisseur. It included natural objects such as shells, but his taste was more for classical sculpture.

OVERLEAF Cabinet of the Dane Ole Worm, from his *Museum Wormianum*, 1655. Worm's education was remarkable. He studied at Aarhus, Lüneberg, Padua, Rome and Naples (where he visited Ferrante Imperato), as well as corresponding with scholars in almost every country of Europe. His cabinet, which is confined to *naturalia*, hardly reflects the range of his knowledge and interests, which included Greek, Latin, physics, medicine, runes and Danish antiquities.

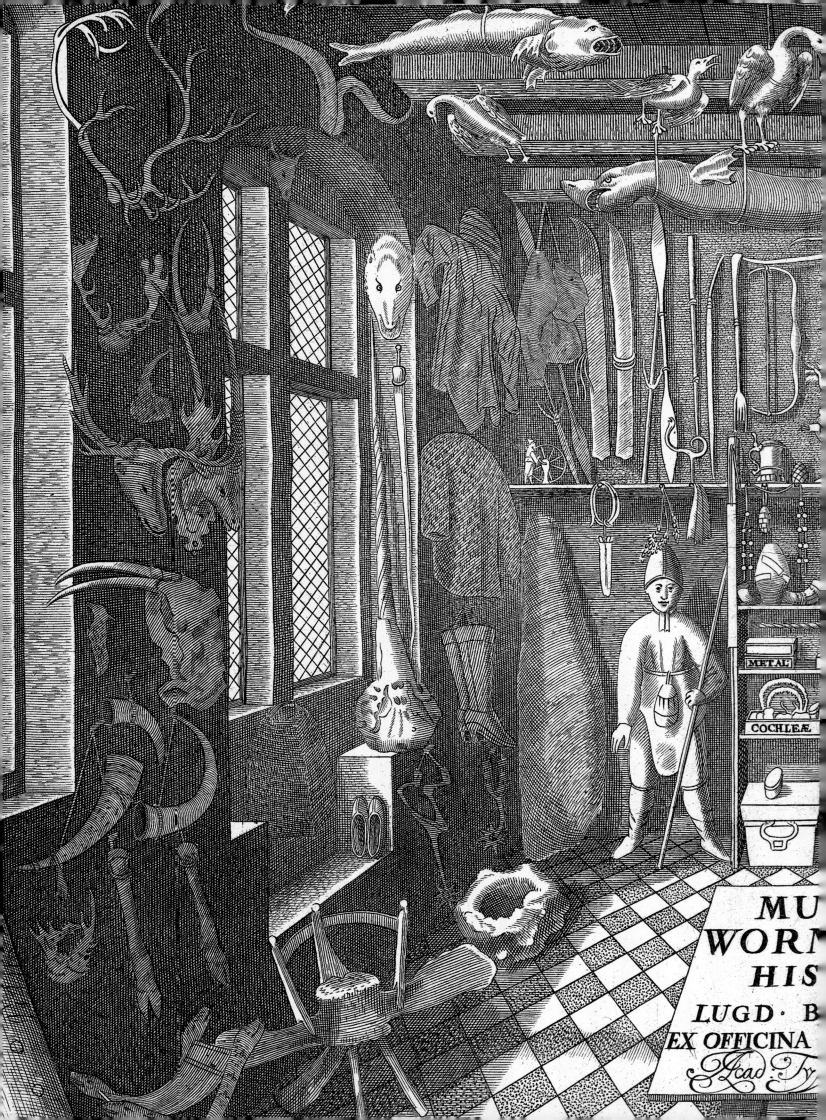

MU
WORM
HIS
LUGD · B
EX OFFICINA
Acad Ty

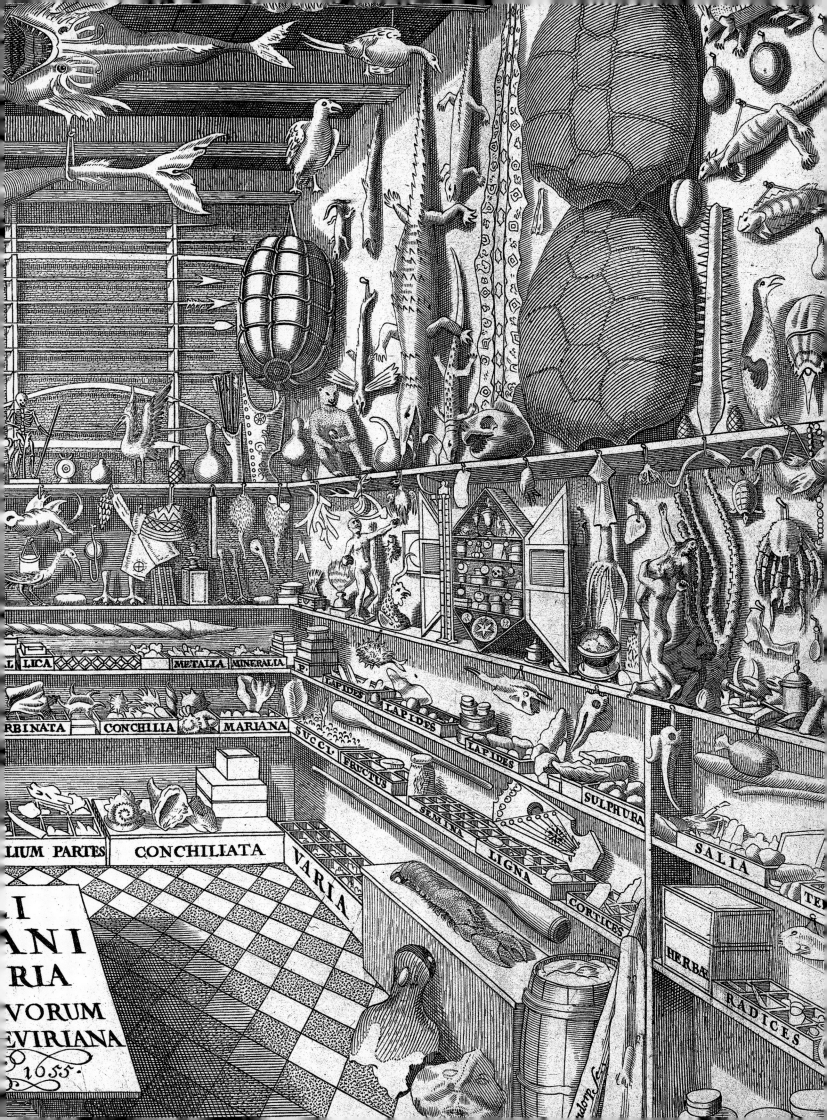

– Montaigne, 'On Solitude'

We should set aside a room, just for ourselves, at the back of the shop, keeping it entirely free and establishing there our true liberty, our principal solitude and asylum. Within it our normal conversation should be of ourselves, with ourselves, so privy that no commerce or communication with the outside world should find a place there; there we should talk and laugh as though we had no wife or children, no possessions, no followers, no menservants, so that when the occasion arises that we must lose them it should not be a new experience to do without them. We have a soul able to turn in on herself; she can keep herself company; she has the wherewithal to attack, to defend, to receive and to give.

The Imperial Library in Vienna in the late 17th century. This view illustrates the way in which books and museum objects were seen as belonging together. Mineral and animal specimens are displayed on the walls and in the cupboards of a room opening off the Library.

BACKGROUND Woodcut from Imperato's *Dell'historia naturale.*

'A theatre of the broadest scope, containing authentic materials and precise reproductions of the whole of the universe': such was the ideal museum of the 1560s, as defined by the Belgian scholar of German adoption Samuel Quiccheberg. At the time when he penned these words, the geography of the cult of curiosities in Europe was still far from attaining the degree of order or hierarchy that it was to attain a century and a half later. Yet a community of purpose did nevertheless unite – across national borders and according to individual means – what might be termed the republic of collectors, who shared the single aim of pinning down the universe in order to 'obtain rapidly, easily and safely a true and unique understanding of the world combined with an admirable wisdom'. It was with this ambitious agenda that Quiccheberg opened his celebrated treatise on museography, *Inscriptiones vel Tituli Theatri Amplissimi* (1565), which was to play a pioneering role in the history of the culture of curiosities in Europe. This was the programme that, with a few minor variations, was to provide the underlying motivation of all those who, from Naples to Copenhagen via Florence or Prague and in ever-increasing numbers from the 1540s, set out to collect, classify and study the world's funds of *artificialia* and *naturalia*, the treasures of art and the wonders of nature.

The modern 'reinventor' of cabinets of curiosities, offering a perspective that bridges the gulf between the sixteenth century and our own, is Julius von Schlosser. In his seminal study devoted to the subject, published in 1908, he draws parallels between these cabinets and the chambers used to house the sacred treasures of Greek temples and later of Christian churches: collections endowed with a special aura, whose magical or supernatural powers have always been linked – more

The Cabinet of Basilius Besler, from his *Fasciculus rariorum varii generis*, Nuremberg, 1622. Besler was another apothecary, whose interests included both animal and plant life. At Eichstätt he was in charge of the botanical garden of Prince-Bishop Konrad von Gemingen, which contained 660 species, many of which Besler drew and published.

ABOVE Engraving from *Fasciculus rariorum varii generis*, Nuremberg, 1622.

or less overtly – to the history of the culture of curiosity (and in the secular sphere extending to include the 'found objects' of the Surrealists). These hidden treasures with their immanent and dangerous power were brought out and displayed to the common gaze only occasionally, just as princes and collectors permitted access to their collections only for brief visits.

It is in this transition from the religious to the secular, from the public (but restricted) treasures of the church to the private (and guarded) treasures of princes, that von Schlosser places the origins of the culture of curiosity; and he finds its embodiment in the person of Jean de Berry, paradigm of all collectors and pioneer in the field of elevating the accumulation and enjoyment of objects to the status of a full-time activity. Von Schlosser viewed northern cabinets of art and curiosities as the expressions of a primarily local spirit linked to the medieval and 'Gothic' (to use his own term) traditions of marvels and miracles. Italian collections, according to his thesis, displayed a tendency by contrast to construct a coherent image of the world, inherited from antiquity and anticipating the modern world view.

It is a distinction that serves a useful purpose in establishing points of reference amid the immense territory covered by the collectors of sixteenth- and seventeenth-century Europe. It also offers helpful typological markers along the way to distinguish the variety of different types of collection that coexisted within this space: collections of ruling kings and lords, secular and religious; collections belonging to scholars, universities or other institutions; and finally the private collections amassed by members of the aristocracy and bourgeoisie, including most notably apothecaries and physicians. But beyond these well-defined categories, there emerged in the century between 1550 and 1650 another, less clearly delineated, area of activity. All recent research devoted to cabinets of curiosities in Italy (A. Lugli), Germany (H. Bredekamp) and France (A. Schnapper) bears out the fact that, until the mid-seventeenth

century, the contrasts that existed between different countries and types of collection were less marked than many historians would have us believe, and that there is a great deal to be gained by turning our attention to the shades of grey in a phenomenon that has hitherto and for many years been interpreted only in starkly simple black and white.

Accumulation, definition, classification: such was the threefold aim of the earliest cabinets of curiosities. Already, the treasure of the abbey church of St Denis offered 'the image of an ordered universe in miniature, with the most prominent relics placed at the centre and surrounded by those of secondary importance'. Arranging his collection to suit himself, Jean de Berry laid it out in innumerable drawers and cabinets, even charging the gaps between the objects with aesthetic significance. In Florence some centuries later, within the 'absolute' space of his *studiolo* in the Palazzo Vecchio (reached through a hidden doorway), Francesco I de' Medici established a subtly modulated dialogue between his paintings and bronzes and his chosen decorative scheme, executed in marble and painted wood around the theme of the four seasons. At Schloss Ambras, finally, Ferdinand of Tyrol's retreat from about 1560, even the colours of the display cabinets were imbued with meaning (blue for crystal vases, green for silverware, red for carved stones, and so on).

The founding secret that lay at the heart of cabinets of curiosities was thus dual in nature: their intention was not merely to define, discover and possess the rare and the unique, but also, and at the same time, to inscribe them within a special setting which would instill in them layers of meaning. Display panels, cabinets, cases and drawers were a response not only to a desire to preserve, or to conceal from view, but also to a parallel impulse to slot each item into its place in a vast network of meanings and correspondences. If the object possessed something of the unique, the rare or the unassimilable, plucked from the infinity of atoms that made up reality, the cabinet would become a place of inspection: a place in which objects were viewed according to a scale, a perspective or a hierarchy that endowed them with meaning – if only on the scale of how fiercely they were desired. This tension found tangible expression, as Adalgisa Lugli has observed,[2] in the external 'packaging' or presentation that was a feature of so many Italian cabinets of curiosities from the Renaissance onwards.

OPPOSITE Woodcut from Gesner's *Thierbuch*, 1563.

OVERLEAF AND FOLLOWING PAGES Perhaps the most complete survival of a cabinet of curiosities is the *Kunst- und Nataralienkammer* at Halle, in Germany. It was begun by August Hermann Francke in 1598. His collection, which was housed in an orphanage, had a teaching purpose. Between 1734 and 1741 it was catalogued and installed in cabinets by Gottfried August Grundler, painter, engraver and naturalist of Halle. (He also financed the first German edition of Linneus's *Systema Natura* in 1740.) The collection grew in the 18th century, enriched partly by donations from former pupils, many of whom travelled worldwide as missionaries. During the 19th century it fell into neglect and was only 'rediscovered' in 1909, when this photograph was taken. It has now been restored to its original glory. Each of the cabinets shown represents a single category, meticulously made and decorated with crowning features reflecting the contents. First: objects from the East – fans, boxes and miniature figures. Second: shells. Third: minerals, fossils and corals and, on the right, various kinds of large nut.

This decorative conceit consisted of panelling in *intarsia* or marquetry which depicted shelves piled high with objects, manuscripts, *mappamundi* and geometrical figures, sometimes glimpsed through doors left ajar. It was another stratum of reality, a *doppelgänger* of the cabinet itself and a *jeu d'esprit* receding to infinity, laying a monochrome veneer of exotic woods over all the chaos of the real world.

Symmetrical displays, symbolic decorative schemes, aesthetically conceived furnishings (cases, cabinets and shelves), *trompe-l'oeil* marquetry: all were devices used by collectors to establish or emphasize the affinities that existed between things, to reveal the fundamental unity that lay beneath this welter of multiplicity. Cabinets were perpetually susceptible to the passion for finding analogies, a theme that belongs as much to the realm of magic as to that of aesthetics, and which haunts the history of the cult of curiosities from its beginnings. Lugli traced it back to the *vis assimilativa*, Nicholas of Cusa's 'force of assimilation' (a human attribute, as opposed to the *vis entificativa*, or creative force, which was divine). Thus through the revelation of hidden connections invisible to the uninitiated, and through the discovery of an essential affinity between objects far removed from each other in geographical origin and in nature, collectors offered their visitors a glimpse of the secret that lay at the heart of all things: that reality is all one and that within it everything has its allotted place, answering to everything else in an unbroken chain. Indeed, Athanasius Kircher had the following inscription painted on the ceiling of his museum: 'Whosoever perceives the *chain* that binds the world below to the world above will know the mysteries of nature and achieve miracles.'[3] This also explained the special place reserved in cabinets of curiosities (as we shall see later) for hybrids (composite creatures, stones in the form of ruins, petrified living things and the like), which by their very nature demonstrated the links that existed between the different natural kingdoms.

It was a view in which symmetry assumed a role of crucial importance. The part it played in the disposition of objects or elements could be likened, in quasi-rhetorical fashion, to an analogy: as a means of drawing distinctions, of apportioning and accentuating secret affinities, it was this principle which, *a priori*, gave the viewer a sense of understanding of what lay before his gaze. Symmetry also established itself as the ruling aesthetic principle governing the settings in which objects were enshrined; for the

PREVIOUS PAGE The Dimpfel family of Regensburg were ironmasters and arms manufacturers. It was probably Johann Paulus Dimpfel (1629–69) who amassed this *Kunstkammer*, painted in 1668, a bourgeois businessman following a princely tradition. This was probably his study and library as well as his museum (there are letters and an inkwell on the table). The objects partly represent his business concerns – model cannon and a suit of armour– as well as a broader range of interests: globes, shells, clocks, Chinese porcelain, antique bronzes, pictures and books.

BACKGROUND The ceiling of the dining room of Scholss Ambras.

cabinet of curiosities was nothing more nor less than a sequence of containers holding within them yet more containers in diminishing order of size, in the ceaseless quest for the allusive essence of a particular realm of knowledge. These boxes and caskets were themselves contained within drawers: drawers which together formed – on an architectural model resembling a monument in miniature – the elements or furnishings of the cabinet of curiosities; cabinets of ebony or ivory, hardstones or tortoiseshell, arranged symmetrically, in their turn, within the space of the chamber. And the space itself, finally, was contained within the engraving that formed the frontispiece to the catalogue of the collection. These spaces, nesting within each other, would then unfold in telescopic fashion around the unique aura of some particular object or other, putting it in perspective for the absent viewer.

Until the time of Elias Ashmole, in the closing years of the seventeenth century, cabinets of curiosities remained associated with a 'mysterious and hierarchical vision of society', fundamentally indebted to the legacy of scholasticism and its allegorical perception of the world.[4] Behind the mystery of each object – unique, fascinating and marvellous – there loomed the shadow of an ancient body of learning, a distant revelation of which the secret had been lost, and which in order to be revealed once more awaited only the meticulous, impassioned gaze of the collector.

The history of cabinets of curiosities is that of a progressive fragmentation, followed by the shattering into kaleidoscopic pieces of these spaces in which every element – from the central table to the cabinet doors, from the window surrounds to the ceiling design – was pressed into service in the pursuit of a single and all-embracing scheme of interpretation and aesthetics. Every aspect of the cabinet of curiosities was hence to become codified and invested with meaning, with analogy and symmetry serving to reinforce the illusion.

One of the true *raisons d'être* behind the growth of cabinets of curiosities was a restless desire to establish a continuity between art and nature.

ABOVE Venetian mirror from Schloss Ambras, 16th century.

OVERLEAF The Dutch artist Hans Jordaens III made a speciality of painting art collectors' galleries. These are nearly all imaginary, though the paintings depicted on the walls may be real. One of them, now in Vienna, illustrates how art-collecting went hand in hand with scientific investigation. The table on the left is piled with the sort of objects that appear in every cabinet of curiosities.

The Cabinet of Manfredo Settala in Milan, from his *Museo…o Galeria*, 1666, one of the richest cabinets of 17th-century Europe. (Settala himself is treated at greater length later in the book, see p. 158). Descended from a line of Milanese doctors, he was both a craftsman (making scientific instruments) and an avid collector of objects of every kind. His annotated catalogue, in seven volumes, was organized thematically. At his funeral in 1680, his coffin was followed by a convoy carrying the most curious items in his museum.

The palatial gallery of Levin Vincent in Amsterdam, from his *Wondertoonel der Nature*, 1706. Vincent's collection was of *naturalia*, including animal specimens preserved in jars, coral, shells and minerals. The plates in his catalogue, of which a supplement was published in 1715, were partly intended as a guide or model for the aesthetic presentation of natural history.

BELOW A cabinet from Vincent's gallery.

– Cesare Vecellio, describing the villa of Odorico Pillone
at Casteldardo, 1590

*He is very learned, grave and witty in his speech,
and there is nothing trivial in his judgments
and opinions, in such a way that all his
actions (which proceed from his very sharp wit)
are by long experience directed towards virtue,
enriched by various doctrines, and resolved by
his perfect judgments. He has a study which
contains many different kinds of book, and is
crammed with every kind of antiquity that one
could desire. There are many ancient medals
and portraits of heroes, and sculptures in
marble and bronze, and there are also fine
natural marvels, so that the study is
appropriately known in that region as the
Ark of Noah, a name given to it by that most
illustrious Cardinal della Torre. So that there is
no-one who passes nearby in the region who
does not want to visit it, as something
marvellous and singular.*

Thus they demonstrate the existence of a supreme unifying principle. As Giuseppe Olmi[5] has observed, this yearning for syncretism, which found its ultimate expression in the taste for the bizarre and the grotesque, reached its culmination in the second half of the sixteenth century, just as the New World began to offer up its inexhaustible supply of 'wonders'. The 'impure' space of the cabinet of curiosities thus attained its finest expression in the closing years of the Renaissance. At this watershed between the Mannerist and the Baroque, the transparent clarity of humanism gave way to a fragmented vision of multiple worlds, both natural and religious, but all preoccupied with the theme – explored in both philosophy and aesthetics – of the fundamentally illusory nature of reality. The history of cabinets of curiosities began with the notion of a correspondence, more or less arcane or magical in nature, between man and nature, between the microcosm and the macrocosm. And it started to disintegrate when this correspondence was revealed as an impossibility, when the ordered space of the cabinet of curiosities lost its claim to reflect the multiplicity of the real world, but could merely boast that it contained a few remnants of it. From this moment, it was no longer possible to embrace creation in all its diversity at a single glance. It was this tension between the desire to exhaust to the full every aspect of the real world, and to contain it within a finite space, and the increasingly clear impossibility of such an undertaking that lies at the heart of the cult of curiosities. It was a task of dizzying scope, akin to the vertiginous attempts of Borges' mapmaker to represent the slightest contours and accidents of the terrain at a scale of one-to-one.

It is possible to be yet more specific in describing the type of space that befitted the pursuit of the cult of curiosities, encompassing the height of the walls, the depth of the furniture, the organization of the space and the arrangement of the objects in the collections, all essential considerations in this context. It is sufficient to draw a contrast between cabinets of curiosities and other types of space already mentioned, which appear to offer a paradigm for them: the politico-religious space, the blind centre of power, represented by the medieval treasury; the aesthetically significant space of the Italian *studiolo*, the cabinets of Renaissance princes; and finally the cabinets of curiosities established by amateur enthusiasts.

OPPOSITE Engravings from Frederik Ruysch, *Thesaurus anatomicus*, Amsterdam, 1701. Above: from Charles de Lecluse, *Exoticorum libri decem*, Leyden, 1605. Below: from Gesner, *Thierbuch*, Zurich, 1563.

OVERLEAF The Imperial collection in Vienna was carefully illustrated in 1730 by Ferdinand Storffer in a sumptuous volume entitled *Specification of those pictures that are to be found in the Black Cabinet and other curiosities in that chest*. The paintings and statues are arranged above the cabinet, but through the glass doors one can see small ivories, birds of paradise and other curiosities.

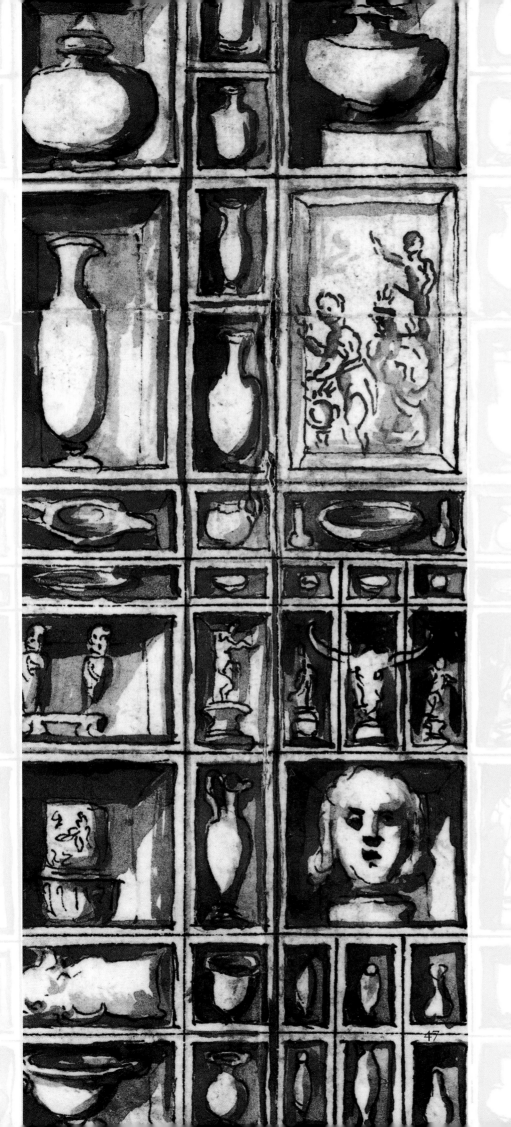

OPPOSITE *Still life with exotic birds* by Isidore Bardi, *c.* 1800.

LEFT The Venetian collector Andrea Vendramin displayed his vases – mostly Greek and South Italian – and antiquities on specially designed wooden shelves. His manuscript catalogue is dated 1627.

OVERLEAF Two paintings of imaginary cabinets.
Left: by Georg Haintz, who lived in Altona, a suburb of Hamburg, around 1666–72. His collection cabinet contains a typical range of natural objects, works of art and *mementi mori*.
Right: A similar imaginary collection by Jean Valette Penot, who worked in Montaubon in the mid-18th century.

The aspects of the medieval treasury that were retained were essentially its symbolic value and its significance as a paradigm: here the object was a sign and token of power, an emblem of sovereignty, whether religious or temporal. Relics jostled with the regalia of power, and together they were invested with a political import that served to guarantee the authority of the figure in whose possession they lay. The German *Kunstkammer*, or cabinet of wonders, was thus prefigured by the *Schatzkammer*, or treasury, though the latter was antithetical in concept. This locked cellar or vault was designed above all to protect and preserve wealth (the royal treasure of the Saxon dynasty, for example, was guarded behind the massive doors of the *grünes Gewölbe*, or 'green vaults', which withstood even twentieth-century bombardments). This was a space whose paradoxical function was to be invisible, to be conspicuous by its absence.

The very term 'cabinet of art and curiosities' came into use only gradually. It was used to designate an enclosed space, often rather cramped and sometimes hidden away, characterized by the singular use it made of the space available and its scholarly array of objects which were brought together primarily to be studied rather than to be put on display. In fourteenth-century France, the precursors of these cabinets were termed *estudes*, and in Italy in the fifteenth and sixteenth centuries they became known as *studioli*. In about 1550, the word *Kunstkammer* ('chamber of art') appeared in German, to be joined soon afterwards by *Wunderkammer* ('chamber of marvels'). In his famous treatise mentioned earlier, Quiccheberg uses both terms, definitively and in conjunction with each other, for the first time: '*Kunstkammer*, that is a close chamber filled with objects fashioned with art (*quod est artificiosarum rerum conclave*), and '*Wunderkammer*, that is a collection of marvellous things (*id est miraculosarum rerum promptuarium*)'. In the late sixteenth century, the two terms merged to form the *Kunst- und Wunderkammer*. And following von Schlosser, this terminology entered the vocabulary of historians writing in every language. Now almost universally

ABOVE AND OPPOSITE Shells from the manuscript catalogue of Ferdinando Cospi.

BACKGROUND From Imperato's *Dell'historia naturale.*

adopted, the German term and its national variations (*cabinet d'art et de curiosité, camera d'arte e di meraviglie*, and so forth) were nevertheless in competition for many years with more widely used designations derived particularly from the realm of theatre (*theatrum mundi, theatrum sapiente*), but also from that of museums, of *promptuaria*, of archives and of cabinets of antiquities, rarities and oddities.

Setting aside such specific distinctions, numerous though they are, the common denominator between these places of study and collection was twofold, lying firstly in the system of organization and eclecticism of the objects amassed, and secondly in the unique personality with which they were imbued. Caught between the two great poles of the wisdom of antiquity, of which the Renaissance sought to achieve a synthesis – nature in its wildest, most untamed forms and art in its boldest manifestations – the objects in these collections arranged themselves within a spectrum of vaulting and universal ambition, the scale of which may be gauged by the categories into which they were divided: *naturalia, mirabilia, artefacta, scientifica, antiquites* and *exotica*. And there was more, including natural history specimens, fossils and botanical and zoological items, both normal and abnormal; paintings, sculpture, gold and silverware, textiles and objects worked in metal, ceramic and leather; and scientific instruments, automata and ethnographical objects. In sum, the personality of each collection depended above all on that of its founder and creator.

It is generally held that, in the closing years of the Middle Ages, cabinets of curiosities took over the representative function of ecclesiastical and royal treasure houses. That the works of art, relics and other remains (sometimes secular) preserved in churches and sanctuaries heralded the collections of works of art and wonders amassed by the humanists. That in their form and in the nature and rarity of the treasures they contained, the *Schatzkammern* (treasure chambers) of medieval royal residences anticipated the collections of the sixteenth century. That there was thus not merely an affinity but rather a direct line of descent from these secular and religious treasure houses to the private museums of the Renaissance. But this continuity – so easy to establish with hind-

OVERLEAF A cabinet in the form of a fantastic tower made in Augsburg in the last quarter of the 16th century for the famous collection of Ferdinand of Tyrol at Schloss Ambras. The materials are alabaster, marble, wood, silver, gilt-bronze and semi-precious stones. The various parts all opened separately, revealing choice items from Ferdinand's collection of coins.

sight – is also doubtless somewhat synthetic. None the less, the turn of the fourteenth and fifteenth centuries saw the growth in France of collections which appear to have served in effect as the link between the medieval accumulations of objects and the ordered cabinets of curiosities that were soon to flourish throughout Europe. The *estudes* of Charles V (1338–80) and above all of his younger brother, the Duc de Berry (1340–1416), were thus to serve as paradigms for later collections. These were cloistered spaces for solitary and secret enjoyment, arranged and presented according to discriminating criteria, with an already discernible but not yet explicit fascination for the twin categories of *naturalia* and *artificialia*. To these the Duc de Berry in particular added a significant nucleus of curiosities, including ostrich eggs, wild boar tusks, mammoth bones, snake skins, amulets to protect against poison, shells and objects with occult powers.

The first cabinets of study and curiosities in the strict sense of the term appeared in northern Italy in the late fifteenth century. Known as *studioli*, these chambers in princely palaces were distinguished by the modesty of their dimensions (rarely exceeding six-and-a-half metres in length), the private and secluded nature of their position within these residences, the richness of their decoration, and the dual nature of the objects contained within them: items symbolizing intellectual striving on the one hand, and works of art and curiosities on the other, with the major – but not exclusive – theme being provided by objects from antiquity; the whole being for the private enjoyment and enlightenment of the prince and his inner circle of friends. The foremost among these *studioli*, in terms of both chronology and celebrity, were those created by Lionello d'Este (1407–50) at the Palazzo Belfiore near Ferrara; by Pietro de' Medici (1414–69) in Florence, a collection notable for its natural curiosities, subsequently inherited by Lorenzo the Magnificent; and by Federico da Montefeltro (1422–82) at the Palazzo Ducale in Urbino. In the early years of the sixteenth century, Isabella d'Este (1474–1539) created her celebrated study chamber and adjoining 'grotto' in the Corte Vecchia of the Palazzo Ducale in Mantua. And a quarter of a century later, one of the most encyclopaedic and

all-embracing *studioli* of the Italian Renaissance, complete with associated workshops and forges, was established in the Palazzo Vecchio in Florence by Francesco I de' Medici (1451–87).

This Florentine example is particularly valuable for more than one reason. Firstly, its creation was contemporary with that of the great dynastic cabinets in countries north of the Alps, so offering the opportunity to test the validity of the contention that cabinets in northern and southern climes were quite different in character. And secondly, the pursuits of its founder – not merely as a collector and connoisseur, but also and more importantly as a craftsman, out of both pleasure and interest – converged with those of other European rulers of the late sixteenth century, all of them eager to experiment with new materials (such as artificial stones, specialized forms of molten glass, weapons and work in gold). Only a matter of a few years separated the creation of Francesco de' Medici's cabinet (1570–5) and that of the *Kunstkammer* in Munich (1563–7), founded at the instigation of Duke Albrecht V of Bavaria (1528–79). A simple comparison of the physical spaces is telling in itself. In the Palazzo Vecchio, the cabinet proper occupied a single room measuring a little over eight metres by three, devoid of either windows or display cabinets, in which the objects were admittedly arranged with care, but behind closed cupboard doors and without any form of identification. This was a place to which the public had no access, and in which each item was the personal property of the collector prince. Albrecht V's *Kunstkammer* in Munich, by contrast, was housed in a separate building, where it

BELOW AND OPPOSITE Two engravings from Aldrovandi's *Monstrorum historia*.

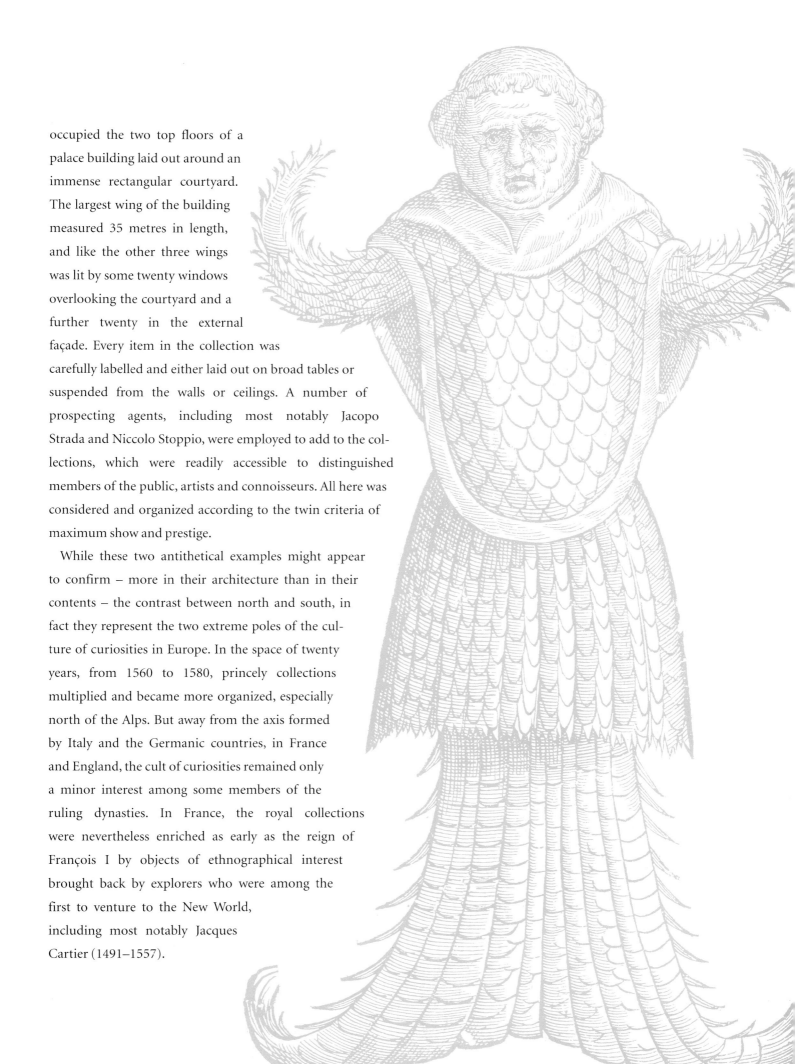

occupied the two top floors of a palace building laid out around an immense rectangular courtyard. The largest wing of the building measured 35 metres in length, and like the other three wings was lit by some twenty windows overlooking the courtyard and a further twenty in the external façade. Every item in the collection was carefully labelled and either laid out on broad tables or suspended from the walls or ceilings. A number of prospecting agents, including most notably Jacopo Strada and Niccolo Stoppio, were employed to add to the collections, which were readily accessible to distinguished members of the public, artists and connoisseurs. All here was considered and organized according to the twin criteria of maximum show and prestige.

While these two antithetical examples might appear to confirm – more in their architecture than in their contents – the contrast between north and south, in fact they represent the two extreme poles of the culture of curiosities in Europe. In the space of twenty years, from 1560 to 1580, princely collections multiplied and became more organized, especially north of the Alps. But away from the axis formed by Italy and the Germanic countries, in France and England, the cult of curiosities remained only a minor interest among some members of the ruling dynasties. In France, the royal collections were nevertheless enriched as early as the reign of François I by objects of ethnographical interest brought back by explorers who were among the first to venture to the New World, including most notably Jacques Cartier (1491–1557).

The arrival of a new *Kunstschrank* (literally 'art-cupboard') was a major event at one of the small German courts. This painting shows the delivery of such a cabinet, accompanied by Philipp Hainhofer of Augsburg, to the court of Philip II, Duke of Pomerania in 1612. Hainhofer was a dealer who made a fortune supplying the courts of Germany with luxury cabinets. This one was destroyed in 1945. Made of walnut, ebony and ivory, it was topped by a silver group of Mount Parnassus, the Nine Muses and the Seven Liberal Arts, and on the lower parts we see the Continents, the Zodiac and the attributes of Man. In other words, the cosmic symbolism of the cabinet mirrors its contents – the universe of Nature, Art and Mind.

A particularly elaborate *Kunstschrank* made in Augsburg about 1625. Made of coloured marbles and ebony, it contains the usual range of objects, natural and artificial, with special emphasis on Christian virtues. When it came into the possession of the Paul Getty Museum a temporary top made of minerals and shells was commissioned from S. Swoboda-Nichols.

FOLDOUT When Gustavus Adolphus entered Augsburg during the Thirty Years War, the city diplomatically presented him with a *Kunstschrank* commissioned by Philipp Hainhofer, now preserved in the University of Uppsala, together with the entire contents. It was a universe in miniature – *naturalia* and *artificialia* (including a clock and even a piano). The opening shows mostly minerals and cameos. The composition of stones, coral and shells that crown it is the work of the goldsmith Johannes Lencher. At the top is a cup of *coca-de-mer* mounted on silver.

By opening another side of Gustavus Adolphus's cabinet, one discovers the so-called 'pharmacy' with drug jars and vessels thought to be prophylactic against poison (right), and (left) toilet items of daily use, including scissors and knives.

At Fontainebleau the same king established a cabinet of 'small curiosities, such as antique medals, silverware, vases, figures, animals, vestments, works from India and foreign Lands, and an infinite number of small favours'. But the history of these collections was not to stretch beyond the 1590s, and Henri IV's ambition to rebuild a *Cabinet de singularitez* under the auspices of the explorer Jean Mocquet was to come to nothing. In England at the same period, historians are unable to identify a single cabinet of art and curiosities even remotely comparable with Continental examples.

The primary purpose of the *studiolo* was to enable its illustrious proprietor to declare his own prestige within an iconographical programme inspired by classical mythology.[6] The interior of the *studiolo* was nonetheless uncluttered; ample space was afforded to works of art, each of which presented a different facet of the overall allegorical meaning. In the most celebrated example, laid out by Francesco de' Medici in the Palazzo Vecchio, the corner statues echo the theme of the four elements depicted in the paintings (the nautical theme of Alessandro Allori's *Pearl Fishers*, for example, is taken up by a statue of Venus by Vincenzo Danti). Beneath this surface theme another meaning lies latent: that of the mastery of nature through the power of art or magic. With its noble themes, the iconographical scheme provides the *studiolo*'s *raison d'être*.

The cabinets of amateur collectors, which succeeded cabinets of curiosities in the second half of the seventeenth century, presupposed a change of scale. Whether they represent depictions of real spaces or – as is more probable – of imaginary settings, the paintings that Franz Francken was to make his speciality offer us an admirable idea of their appearance. The lofty walls of these spacious rooms are covered with paintings (each meticulously rendered and perfectly recognizable in a technical *tour de force*), hung in a spirit that seems to anticipate that of modern art galleries. On a table in the foreground lies a collection of medals, corals, symbols of human vanity, gemstones, shells, fossils and the like, which a century earlier would have furnished a cabinet of curiosities. But this collection, which would have made up the whole of an earlier cabinet, here forms only a part of the painting, and of the gallery; the former now appears, within the confines of the latter, which contains it in every sense of the word. In a corner of the image, meanwhile, a glimpse of a garden or another room offers a context to the arrangement within the room, and a fresh perspective on it.

OPPOSITE A writing box of silver, partly gilt, enamel, velvet, silk, rock-crystal and ebony by Wenzel Jamnitzer of Nuremberg, 1502. The figure is an allegory of Philosophy, and the tablet she is holding reads: 'Science restores to memory things that have passed away, erects lasting monuments of art and brings back into the light that which had fallen into darkness.'

A century later and in a different setting both historically and geographically, the cabinet of Joseph Bonnier de la Mosson, as depicted by Jacques de Lajoue (see p. 184), emphasizes the prime importance of the décor. Here it is the architecture of the room and its decorative scheme – its scale and proportions, the elegance of its lines, the design of its woodwork and the grace of its scrolls and arabesques – that provide the dominant impression, fixing the viewer's gaze before it has time to stray over the contents of the collections, which are now distributed among display cabinets devoted to specialized fields such as optics, natural sciences, geography and so forth. Here the interior is presented as a skilfully arranged composition, light, airy and almost insubstantial; this is a space in which to study the natural sciences and the objects of the collection with the detached, dispassionate eye of a dilettante.

Though the setting might vary, the space within the cabinet of curiosities was largely allocated according to an unchanging formula. With every corner and niche filled to overflowing, and every surface studded from floor to ceiling with a carapace of precious and rare objects, it was unable by its very nature to display all the treasures that it contained (hence the need to multiply its space with the use of as many different surfaces, tabletops and drawers as possible). This was a private space, requiring a formal introduction in the ritual form of the visit, as described by cultivated travellers from Montaigne to John Evelyn: a display ceremony in which the cult of the object was celebrated, and its history, its origins and its fabulous genealogy were unveiled to the faithful in a form of ecstatic communion.

Cramming together so many objects within such a confined space had the effect of creating a dizzying foreshortening of the perception. As well drawing attention to analogies of form and surface similarities, this also had the even more striking effect of throwing into sharp relief the unique qualities of each piece and the marvellous variety of each collection.

Viewed from a psychological standpoint, this overwhelming profusion of objects offers eloquent clues not only to the history of each collection (presenting us with a synoptic vision of an endeavour that was necessarily scattered over time), but also and more importantly to the constant, insatiable need to add, to complete, to gather together, to leave no gap unfilled. It speaks of the cyclical nature of the lust to possess and the satisfaction of possession, of the unfinished work in progress and the completed collection. These surfaces crowded with objects, frozen in their serried ranks and undeviating symmetry, are also curiously eloquent, imparting still a burning, impatient, feverish quality which undoubtedly accounts for their continuing and undiminished power to fascinate.

At the same time, they also set out deliberately to produce an effect on the viewer: to impress him with the sheer lavishness and opulence of this cornucopia, before leading him from one object to the next, each more bizarre or wonderful than the last. For wonder was the keynote of the cabinet of curiosities, and the marvels of the collection, in all their far-flung historical and geographical variety, were the fundamental components.

The first impression on entering a cabinet
of curiosities was one of a world in
miniature, an accumulation of objects in
such profusion that it was difficult to find
one's way round it; there was no beginning
and no end. But the visitor was then expected
to open the cupboards and the drawers
and to examine each object in detail.
LEFT A shell cup carried by a triton whose
arms are imprisoned in the mount. Made
at the end of the 16th century by an
unknown artist, it is now in Vienna.

OVERLEAF A vivid evocation of what such cabinets
contained, indicative of the extraordinary range of
interests that motivated the collector. Known as the
Yarmouth Collection, it was commissioned by
the Paston family about 1665, probably from a Dutch
artist, to record some of its treasures. There are
animal and mineral specimens, works of art, musical
instruments, a globe, an hourglass, two nautilus
cups, one with musical satyrs, and allusions to
exotic cultures in the African holding a monkey.

Naturalia and artificialia

In cabinets of curiosities as in any other collection, the presence of any particular object was justified, *a priori*, by its rarity. It was a rarity that might be purely contingent (when the item in question was one of the last surviving parts of a series, for instance); or it might concern its origins, whether in time (as with relics) or in space (as with ethnographic objects); or it might derive from its exceptional workmanship (as with pieces of finely worked gold, turned ivory and the like).

It was this exceptional quality that justified the admission of the object into the collection, and which in dialectic fashion vindicated the existence of the latter, newly validated as it was with each fresh acquisition. A certain school of psychological thought recognizes in this craving for the unique the basic impulse that drives all collectors: the need to see reflected in the objects of their collections an exhilarating, narcissistic projection of their own self-image.

This quest for rarity among curiosities had the effect of escalating the degree of singularity required of items in ordinary collections: henceforth only the unique would suffice, the idiosyncratic pushed to the point of incongruity. Aberrations and freaks were now eagerly sought in each of the two kingdoms into which creation was divided: *naturalia* and *artificialia*.

Cabinets of curiosities accordingly set out to establish the contiguity of these two realms, each shot through in its turn by the category of 'marvels' or 'wonders, and which could be both natural and man-made.

Minerals were collected both for their scientific value and for their beauty: the two concepts were not, indeed, easily distinguishable.

OPPOSITE Ammonite and stones from the Halle collection (a detail of p. 27).

LEFT In 1581 the Emperor Rudolf II gave Augustus the Strong, Elector of Saxony, a piece of virgin rock in which were embedded sixteen emeralds, of some great size (only ten remain). It came from Colombia in South America. The Elector commissioned the sculptor Balthasar Permozer to make a setting for it in the form of a South American Indian, adding other jewels on his body: rubies, sapphires, topaz, garnets and tortoiseshell.

BACKGROUND Woodcut from Aldrovandi's *Museum metallicum*, 1648.

RIGHT A mask of jade, probably from Central America, acquired by the Medici.
The mount is of gold, enamel and diamonds, *c.* 1650–60.

OPPOSITE The Medici became increasingly fascinated by grottoes. That at Castello contains two large-scale reliefs depicting animals which seem to grow out of the rocky cave. Each animal is carved from a different stone; the sculptor is said to have been Giambologna.

BELOW A stone cup, late 16th-century Italian; made for the Medici.

BACKGROUND from Besler's *Fasciculus rariorum varii generis*, 1622.

OVERLEAF Two ingenious ways of submitting beautiful minerals to the human imagination. Left: One of the panels in the open doors of the Uppsala Cabinet (pp. 59–62). The veined marble has become a sort of mystic landscape through which visionary armies move. Right: Florentine artists developed a technique for using minerals (*pietra dura,* 'hard stone') to make pictures.

SHELLS: LIFE DEPARTED

Shells, creations of life and nature, had a powerful appeal to the Mannerists, with their exotic shapes and colours that no artist could have invented, and their suggestion of another world that was wholly inhuman yet darkly symbolic, slightly sinister but irresistibly beautiful.
RIGHT: *Shells* by Bartolomeo Bimbi.

OPPOSITE Grand Duke Francesco I of Tuscany was keenly interested in natural phenomena, including alchemy. In his *studiolo* in the Florentine Palazzo Vecchio, a claustrophobic little room filled with paintings, he could commune with these subjects brought to life by some of the most brilliant Mannerist artists of the day. Many of them feature minerals and gems, with the classical and allegorical figures associated with them. Allesandro Allori painted *Pearl Fishers* (detail), revelling not only in the bodies of the fishers and their pearls but also in the bizarre shapes of the shells from which they came.

BACKGROUND from Besler's *Fasciculus rariorum varii generis*, 1622.

– Charles Patin, Travels through Germany, *1696*

There are also Rocks beset with Pearls and rich Stones; and in short, the Jewels of this nature are so numerous that this Press alone is an inestimable Treasure. In the next cabinet are preserv'd Urns of red Earth, and others of Porcelane of China *and* Japan, *among which are observ'd some counterfeit; they are the common ones that come from* Holland, *which have been put in vogue on purpose to save a greater expense.*

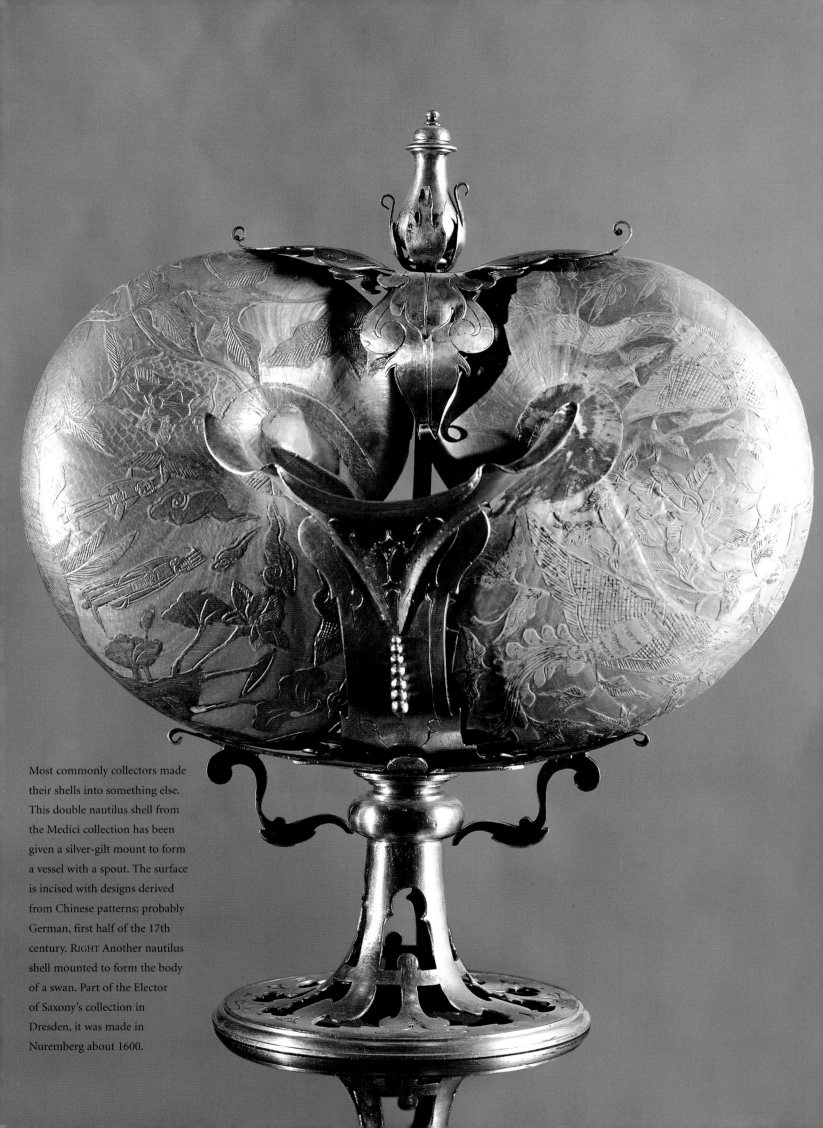

Most commonly collectors made
their shells into something else.
This double nautilus shell from
the Medici collection has been
given a silver-gilt mount to form
a vessel with a spout. The surface
is incised with designs derived
from Chinese patterns; probably
German, first half of the 17th
century. RIGHT Another nautilus
shell mounted to form the body
of a swan. Part of the Elector
of Saxony's collection in
Dresden, it was made in
Nuremberg about 1600.

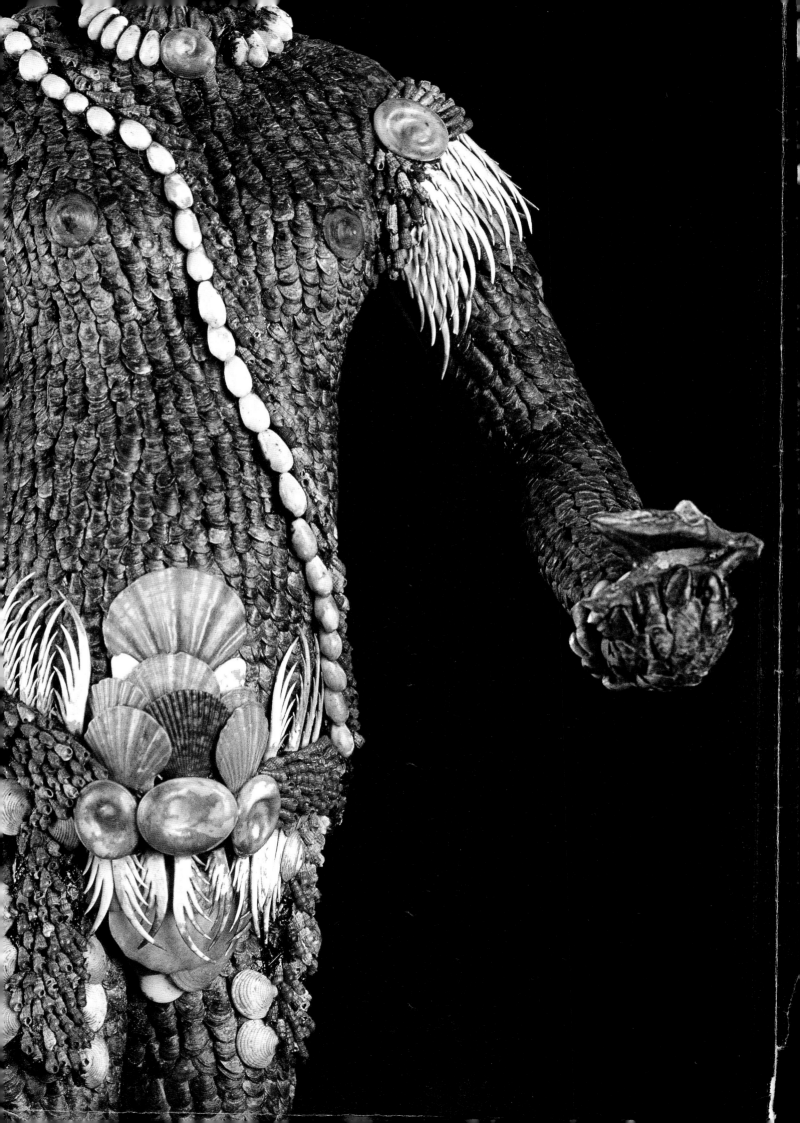

In 1683 Cosimo III, Grand Duke of Tuscany, presented a collection of shells and minerals to the marchese Ferdinando Cospi of Bologna. A manuscript catalogue with meticulous illustrations by Giacomo Tosi was compiled. One of the plates shows how the shells were displayed.

FOLDOUT The Medici of Florence were keen collectors of shells, arranging them in a variety of ingenious ways, none more amazing than those on these pages. The close-up heads consist of shells on a papier mâché base; the full figures have a wooden base. They reflect contemporary interest in distant places; there were certainly African slaves at the Florentine court, probably from the kingdom of the Congo. They also reflect a knowledge of Arcimboldo (p. 129), who had virtually invented the art of making human beings out of other materials.

CORAL:
BETWEEN LIFE AND DEATH

Coral consists of the accumulated skeletons of tiny sea-creatures, the deposits of which form shapes resembling plant growth. It was thus of particular fascination for collectors, since it seemed to combine animal, mineral and vegetable. In Ferdinand II's cabinet at Schloss Ambras (1550–75) the specimens were arranged on plaster brackets. ABOVE An ostrich-egg mounted on a silver-gilt ostrich and ornamented with coral above and below; made in Augsburg by Clement Kicklinger, 1570–75. BELOW Coral pendant in a gold setting with precious stone inlay.

Thus artistic masterpieces and virtuoso examples of technical skill jostled with evidence of divine omnipotence (such as marvels of nature, relics and the earthly vestiges of miracles). Together these two realms formed one complete world, or microcosm, which was a reflection of the macrocosm and of creation in general. If the world could be contained in a single room, it was because no natural object was devoid of significance, but rather everything was a manifestation of a plan or a latent meaning. Everything, concluded the rhetorician Emanuele Tesauro, was a metaphor, 'and if nature speaks to us through these metaphors, it follows that an encyclopaedic collection, as the sum of all possible metaphors, must logically become the all-encompassing metaphor for the world.'[7] The collector, meanwhile, played the part of a master-mind bringing these two chains of being together.

From the earliest appearance of cabinets of curiosities towards the mid-sixteenth century, the echoes and reverberations between these twin poles thus assumed a role of fundamental importance. Cabinets were distinguished by the emphasis each placed on a particular type of object, while at the same time being united in their essential aim of teasing out the metaphor of a seamless creation. While the cabinets of the apothecaries Ulisse Aldrovando and Ferrante Imperato were noted for their outstanding collections of 'natural' objects, that of Rudolf II lay at the opposite extreme, being remarkable above all else for its sweeping embrace of all forms of being and every manner of object and device. Two tendencies rapidly emerged. One was the scientific endeavour of amassing objects that would offer a corresponding variety of matters for analysis.

The coexistence of art and science is made explicit in this display of coral and shells (opposite) from Levin Vincent's *Wundertoneel der Natur* (1706). The upper section is arranged as decoration, while the drawers contain other specimens stored for scholarly research.

LEFT Two drinking cups by Eberhard Lindeman, early 17th-century, made in Torgau, part of the Dresden collection.

Two more coral examples of *naturalia* transformed into *artificialia*. LEFT To escape the attentions of Apollo, Daphne prayed to be turned into a laurel-bush, a subject that has attracted artists at all times. Wenzel Jamnitzer, about 1550, uses coral to represent the hands that are being transformed into branches. RIGHT In an elaborate 'grotto' in the collection of Ferdinand of Tyrol at Schloss Ambras, coral is used to represent rocks, trees, the Three Marys, Christ, the Thieves and the crosses on which they were crucified.

The other was the magico-theological ambition of reflecting creation in all its variety and diversity. This aesthetic of the hybrid, expressed as a desire to mingle art and nature and to seek their progeny in the bizarre and the grotesque, grew in influence (it is generally agreed) in the second half of the sixteenth century, encouraged, as has been seen, by the opening up of the New World and its inexhaustible fund of the outlandish.

Aldrovandi's intention, as summed up by A. A. Shelton, [8] 'was not to celebrate the symmetry and harmony of the divine order', but rather to verify the relativist notion that, through the possibilities and materials it presented, the environment was a conditioning factor in human customs and cultures. Antonio Giganti, a secretary to the bishop of Bologna, by contrast assembled a collection which 'juxtaposed like with unlike aspects, which meant that groups of objects were arranged together in his collections in accordance with particular themes. The symmetry by which he arranged and grouped objects was conceived as inherent in nature: it mirrored the harmonious unity of the world.'

This opposition between two types of collection, and by extension between the items therein, may be likened to the contrasts between the different types of discourse (humble or scholarly, vernacular or Latin, informative or rhetorical) and culture ('high' or 'low') that were such a determining influence at this period, remaining so into the modern era. The different registers of medieval rhetoric were thus transposed into the field of painting, an essential element of the realm of *artificialia*, where they were diligently repeated. This explains why Rudolf II's cabinet contained two types of painting which were apparently mutually exclusive, to both of which he attached importance.

WAX: THE SHADOW OF LIFE

Coloured wax could – and still can – actually deceive the eye into mistaking artifice for reality; and it was this very borderline that fascinated the collector of curiosities. In conjunction with naturalistic painting, real clothes and real hair the illusion could indeed be startling. RIGHT A wax picture of Duke Frederick II of Gotha, *c.* 1700. The figure was recently re-clothed in authentic fabrics.

OPPOSITE A series of wax faces modelled on death-masks that formed part of the Halle collection (see pp. 26–31). Those on the top shelf are dressed as in life; those at the bottom, even more unnervingly, are shown as corpses in their coffins with eyes closed.

One of the most important royal collections was that of Denmark, housed at Copenhagen in the castle of Rosenborg. It was begun by Christian IV around 1660 and was always stronger in jewelry, works of art and craftsmanship than in *naturalia*. These two very lifelike wax busts are of the future King Frederick VI (left) and his childhood playmate, an orphan called Carl, both aged about three.

On the one hand the exaggerated Mannerism, formal refinement and sophisticated eroticism of a painter such as Spranger, and on the other the resolute naturalism and rejection of all idealization of an artist such as Roelandt Savery, exponent of the new genre painting. Poised at opposite ends of the artistic spectrum, these two schools of painting represented two 'modes' or registers, the coexistence of which was essential to the balance and dynamics of the cabinet as a whole.[9]

RIGHT Details from Besler's *Fasciculus rariorum varii generis*, 1622.

One way of making living things into collectable objects was to cast them in metal, and this became a highly sophisticated skill. This silver-gilt crocodile (below), German, 1575–1600, was a sand-container.

The emphasis that had hitherto been placed on the natural sciences now shifted to a vision of the world that was above all allegorical or symbolic. And within any collection of the latter type, attention was now turned to the notion of the relative nature of things, to the concept of the chains of being to be found within art and nature, and to a belief in hidden affinities. To those who held contrary beliefs, meanwhile, or who dismissed the notion of an invisible order as unverifiable, it was the object *per se*, irreducible and unique in every way, that justified the collection's existence. In both instances, however, the object was defined – albeit according to differing values – by a single essential property that derived from its rarity: it was both the embodiment and the vehicle of the phenomenon that was fundamental to the cabinet of curiosities, that of 'wonders' or 'marvels'.

LIFE ARRESTED

OVERLEAF Even closer to real life was to make scale models of insects and small animals in papier mâché. A shallow box made for Ferdinand II at Ambras contained such replicas of small bugs and snails with jointed heads and limbs, so that when the box was shaken they moved as if they were alive.

There is nothing better worth seeing than the collection of Signor Septalla, a canon of St Ambrose, famous over Christendom for his learning and virtues. Amongst other things, he showed us an Indian wood, that has the perfect scent of civet; a flint, or pebble, that has a quantity of water in it, which is plainly to be seen, it being clear as agate; divers crystals that have water moving in them, some of them having plants, leaves, and hog's bristles in them, much amber full of insects, and divers things of woven amianthus.

OPPOSITE Wenzel Jamnitzer's ewer, made in Nuremberg about 1570, uses a Trochus shell for the main vessel, but stands on a silver-gilt mount of an eagle attacking a snail. The eagle is an artwork, but the snail is cast from life.

ABOVE Another cast from nature, an eagle's claw supporting a nautilus cup; German, late 16th-century.

BELOW Box for a writing-set by Wenzel Jamnitzer. The sides and the compartments of the lid are silver casts of living things – herbs, grasses, lizards, a shell, a grasshopper and a frog. It was made about 1570 for Ferdinand II's cabinet at Ambras.

Truly dead things could still be given the illusion of life by preservative techniques. LEFT Part of Levin Vincent's collection, published in 1706; it shows jars of fluid containing various small animals, frogs and snakes. Inset in the middle is a real baby's head, made more lifelike by the bizarre addition of a lace cap. BELOW A crocodile embryo in a jar from the Halle collection.

Frogs in jars (this page background and opposite) are from the cabinet of Frederik Ruysch.

LIFE INVENTED

The mythology of dragons and mermaids – half women, half fish, who lured men to their doom – goes back to classical times. The early scientists, with no foolproof method of distinguishing fact from fiction, were inclined to give credence to these stories, and if evidence was lacking there was a temptation to manufacture it. RIGHT A bronze dragon by Severo Calzetta da Ravenna, *c.* 1500. BELOW The not-too-convincing skeleton of a mermaid, from an Italian cabinet.

– Charles Patin, Travels through Germany, *1690*

In the same Place are kept divers Mummies of all sorts, and as these kinds of Curiosities are not very useful; so neither are they destitute of their peculiar Beauty: Of these some are White and others Black, but the later are generally embalm'd, wrapt up in Swathing-bands, and beset with Idols or the Images of small Animals and other superstitious Embellishments. I was elsewhere presented with some Rarities of this kind which were lately dugg out of the Ground under a Pyramid in Ægypt.

Mirabilia

The extraordinary cabinet presented as a tribute to the Swedish king Gustav Adolphus by the town of Augsburg on 22 April 1632 – constructed from oak and ebony; inlaid with marble, agate, enamel and silver; and crowned with crystals, coral and shells – contained among other items an anamorphic drawing, a ewer fashioned from a nautilus shell, a selection of mathematical instruments, a musical clockwork mechanism, and a mummified monkey's paw.[10] Amid this apparently eclectic array, the objects nevertheless shared one common feature: each created art out of nature (as in the nautilus shell with its silver mounts), or rather merged the two to the point where they became indistinguishable, in a mutual exchange of properties and an absolute quality of perfection that could not fail to discountenance or disorientate the viewer. This transgression, this breaching of the opposition between the two mutually exclusive realms of creation, found its natural expression in the bewilderment of the astonished observer, and was the true source of the sense of wonder.

These were objects that forged a link between two orders of reality where none existed, and which did so moreover for no apparent purpose and with a level of sophistication that appeared impossible to justify; objects that truly defied understanding. They gave physical expression, in so many minor epiphanies, to different idioms of the marvellous that could be analysed and described. One of the most immediately striking was undoubtedly abrupt changes of scale, playing on the effects of miniaturization and magnification: the disruption, in the most direct way possible, of customary points of reference, of the accepted scale of things, and of all that made up the familiar world of the viewer. Into this category came the remains, whether real or imagined, of prehistoric or fabulous creatures and objects, including giants' footsteps, emeralds of prodigious size and elephants' tusks. At the other extreme, many collectors of cabinets of curiosities had a fondness for dwarves: they provided an added attraction to the gallery of contrasts in Rudolf II's collection, and in Manfredo Settala's 'museum' acted as guides. Here they also served as exhibits in a way, being counted among the marvels of the collection and recorded for posterity in an engraving of the collection: a wonder that lay somewhere between the inanimate objects and life itself.

DEATH PROLONGED

Just as living things were preserved in death, so death was brought to life. This has a long history in Baroque art and from there was absorbed into the world of curiosities. Even the anatomist Vesalius posed his skeletons in elegant and thoughtful poses, often occupied in some everyday activity. One of the engravings from his *De Humani corporis fabrica* (1555) was copied by Paul Reichel for his *memento mori* cabinet in the Ambras collection. The skeleton contemplates a book, an hourglass and bow and arrow. Background on this page: Death as hunter, woodcarving by Hans Leinberger, 1520–30.

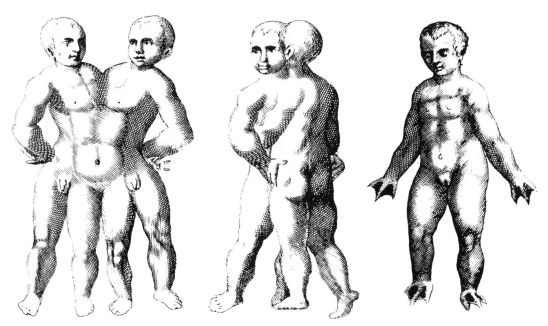

Nature deformed

From the monsters of folklore and mythology to the freaks of real life was no very long step. Both excited wonder and – in some cases – an undoubtedly morbid curiosity. The hydrocephalic baby (opposite) was one of the exhibits in jars of Dr. Ruysch, whose collection was later the nucleus of Peter the Great's *Kunstkammer* in St Petersburg. The Siamese twins were drawn by Fortunio Liceti in his *Monstrorum Cassis* and the even more shocking example (below) by Ulisse Aldrovandi.

– John Evelyn at Leiden, 1641

But, amongst all the rarities of this place, I was much pleased with a sight of their anatomy-school, theatre, and repository adjoining, which is well furnished with natural curiosities; skeletons from the whale and elephant to the fly and spider, which last is a very delicate piece of art. Amongst a great variety of other things, I was shown the knife newly taken out of a drunken Dutchman's guts, by an incision in his side, after it had slipped from his fingers into his stomach.

Monstrous births of the animal
world. ABOVE A three-headed
sheep by Liceti. RIGHT Two-
headed lamb by Bartolomeo
Bimbi. As often in Bimbi's
paintings, he provides
scientific information as well.

OVERLEAF Engravings
from *Fasciculus rariorum
varii generis* and Aldrovini's
Monstrorum historia.

o Febb.º 1720. ab In:ᵉ in Giouedì a tre
otte, in un podere della Priᵒ:ⁱᵃ di S.Ang
prefente Agnello bianco marauigliofo
ue Tefte, e due Colli con i fuoi Efofaghi,
l'interiora, che aueua tenendo due Polmo
due Milze, due Cuori, raddoppiati i
l'Inteftini, i quali andauano po a termi
. Aueua due foli Lombi, et una fola

Continuing in the realm of differences and aberrations of scale, miniature objects in general played an indispensable role in any collection of wonders: offering an unaccustomed perspective on the visual world, they were also invariably the product of a technical *tour de force* of breathtaking complexity and skill. The collections of Schloss Ambras, for example, contain a wooden writing case measuring a mere 44 centimetres, consisting of a veritable forest of turrets and pillars. Items in turned ivory provided consummate examples of the genre, unrivalled in their intricacy and diminutive scale.[11] The rigging of a frigate carved in ivory by an artist at the court of Hesse in 1620 is so delicate, meanwhile, as to be untouchable. Reduced in scale, inward-looking and cocooned within themselves, these prodigies seem to contain infinity, to reach to the very limits of the visible. Thus we may marvel before ninety-six goblets that fit precisely one into the next, or attempt to count the hundred heads engraved on a cherry stone, or the twenty-four minuscule spoons concealed within another cherry stone.[12] Each tinier than the last and contained within it, these virtuoso exercises in the art of miniaturization are another demonstration of the general rule of containment and encapsulation, of treasures nestling one within the other, that was the governing principle of cabinets of curiosities.

Add to these the items that were traditionally *de rigueur* in cabinets of curiosities, such as unicorns' horns, bezoars, mandragora, birds of paradise, petrified wood and coral branches, and ultimately it is reality that seems to dissolve into a rhetorical chimaera, swirling in the mists of improbability, carried away by a 'taste for the complex, the obscure, the marvellous, the extravagant; a heady penchant for artifice and all that is novel and protean […], a propensity for excess and ostentation; the declaration of the supremacy of sight over the other senses'.[13]

The juxtaposition of versions of reality that lay at the most distant or disparate extremes was a rhetorical exercise *par excellence*, as we have seen. It found its counterpart in another class of objects deemed truly marvellous, including antlers growing out of a tree trunk (purchased by Ferdinand II in 1563 for Schloss Ambras)[14] or the outline of a cat in a marble plaque in Aldrovandi's collection.[15] Hybrids now made their appearance once more as one of the most fundamental sources of

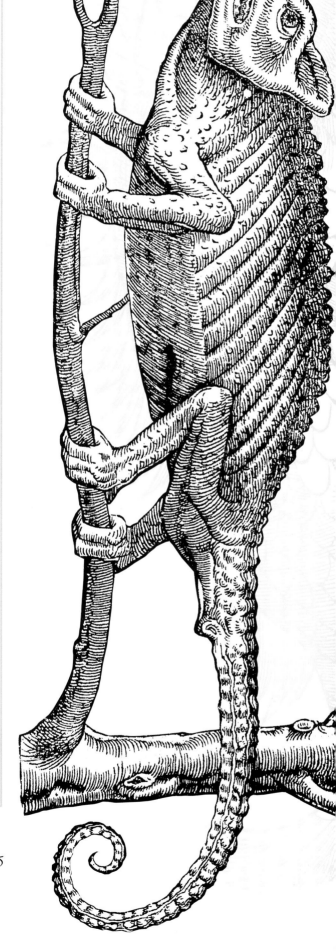

– Conrad Gesner, 1551

And this rule must be followed in looking into the nature of beasts: for we ought to enter into their consideration without fear or blushing, seeing the operation of nature is everywhere very honest and beautiful, for therein is nothing done inconsiderately and without a true end, but all things advisedly for a certain and determinate purpose, and this purpose doth alway contain both both goodness and honesty. But if any man be so barbarous as to think that the beasts and such other creatures cannot afford him any subject worthy of his contemplation, let him think so of himself likewise; for what ignoble baseness is there in blood, flesh, bones, veins and such like? Doth not the body of man consist thereof? And then how abhominable art thou to thyself that thou dost not look into these which are so near of kind unto thee?

AUTOMATA

An automaton – a non-living thing that moves – falls into the same ambivalent category that we have encountered so often before; the line separating life from death. What might now seem to be merely clockwork toys could then raise profound philosophical issues. BELOW A 16th-century German *automaton* of Neptune sitting on a tortoise, both of which can move.

OPPOSITE 'The chained slave', probably made by Manfredo Settala himself (see p. 158). The mechanism was activated by the weight of the unsuspecting visitor to the museum, so that the head (by a technique similar to the practical jokes of some Baroque gardens) started to make threatening screams and movements. The body and face of the wooden figure present a sharp contrast of style, the former modelled on classical prototypes, the latter following a more grotesque popular tradition.

wonder, for the simple reason that they challenged accepted systems of classification and the limits of the visible world, so undermining the very foundations of reality.

Automata

Hybrids between art and nature or the 're-creation' by nature of artistic forms; or cult of the extraordinary, with the power to overturn established norms, amaze the onlooker and arouse wonder: these are the twin threads that we have now teased out in the history of the cult of curiosities. To them should now be added a third, or rather – and more significantly – another pair of opposites.

Other items most likely to have found a place in cabinets of curiosities included wax portraits, dried or pressed flora, stuffed animals and automata: examples of borderline or hybrid cases, once again, but this time united at least by a common property. 'Truer than life', they belonged to a world that lay within a hair's breadth of that of appearances, of the semblance of life, of the realm of chimaeras and the art of the illusionist. Feigning life in the lifeless, they appeared to signal the triumph of life over death, defy categorization in either camp, and holding out the promise of prolonged or eternal life in an improbable but none the less tangible world beyond.

A similar vision is more or less implicit in the hermetic tradition, that is in the system of correspondences that provided the inspiration for most cabinets of curiosities. Behind the dialogue and the play of analogies between artistic and natural forms lay the greater theme of a universal system of correspondences, in which all things were united in a single Oneness or cosmos, every element of which found its echo in another. Microcosm and macrocosm, high and low, animate and inanimate, living and dead: all

found their reflection and were made complete in this universal response. Thus the collector, in much the same way as a sorcerer or alchemist, became the master or manipulator of the pulsing forces that ebbed and flowed silently across the real world: the aura of a star, the energy of a body that appeared dead, the power of a talisman, astrological influences and the inspiration of plants and minerals. Marshalling these secret impulses in the private theatre of his cabinet, the collector was never far from the realm of necromancy, engaged as he was in bringing the dead back to life or consigning living things to death. The funereal connotations of so many of the items central to the cult of curiosities – from mummified limbs to coral branches, from the mythical congealed blood of the Medusa to stuffed animals, from skulls to a charnel house of other bones – were ultimately not only the most superficial expression of this theme, but also the most morbidly fascinating.

This dialectic between life and death, this infatuation with the aesthetic transfiguration wrought by death, recurs at an even deeper level, informing the very organization of the collection. It is central, indeed, to the thesis underlying the cabinet of curiosities: for the aim of any collection is to halt the passage of time, to freeze the ineluctable progress of life or history, and to replace it with the fragmented, controllable, circular time frame established by a finite series of objects that can be collected in full. Subordinated to the general order of things, this time frame delineates an island of sense amid an ocean devoid of meaning. While all collections are concerned with the dialectic between 'disappearance' and 'survival', cabinets of curiosities elevated this obsession to a higher and more rigorous level. Not only did they bring together objects that had eluded or survived the test of time – in itself a cause of wonder – but they also brought together hybrid, liminal objects (suspended between art and nature, death and life), so investing them with new value, new power and new meaning. Like the hero of the Edgar Allen Poe story, the objects in the cabinet of curiosities seem to oscillate perpetually between life and death, returning to life in death, and occupying an eternal no man's land between the two.

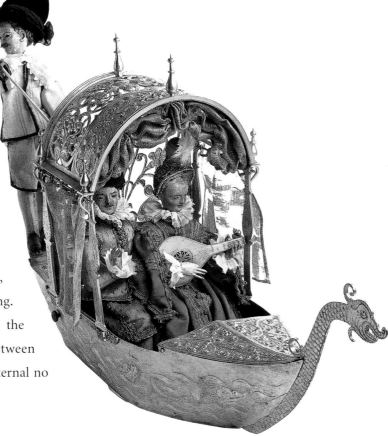

OPPOSITE A clock in the form of Diana riding on a centaur, made in silver, enamel, precious stones and wood by Melchior Maier of Augsburg about 1605. The centaur rolls its eyes and fires an arrow; Diana and one of her dogs move their heads; the other dog opens its mouth.

BELOW A musical gondola from the Ambras collection, *c.* 1600. It moves on wheels, its direction governed by the gondolier at the back. The lady with the lute sings; the man moves his arm.

Two clocks in Copenhagen
with ingenious supplementary
mechanisms, both by Josias
Habrecht of Strasbourg, the
astronomical clock (left) of 1594;
the armillary sphere of 1572.
The four faces register hours,
quarter hours, latitude and the
planets for each day. It is said
to have been acquired by the
astronomer Tycho Brahe.

MIRACLES IN IVORY

The extraordinary feats of 16th- and 17th-century craftsmen in ivory can still provoke gasps of incredulous amazement. Most cabinets contained examples of these wonders of ingenuity; the Dresden collection held over two hundred, including the four shown here (opposite). The one on this page is Florentine. The ambition was to carve one shape *inside* another, and another inside that as many times as one could. Rudolf II himself practised the art.

BACKGROUND From Jamnitzer's *Perspectiva Corporum Regularium*, 1568.

Ivory-carving was nourished by the contemporary obsession with perspective and solid geometry. This cabinet, made in South Germany at the end of the 16th century, derives directly from Renaissance studies in perspective, for instance those of Dürer. In 1568 Wenzel Jamnitzer published his *Perspectiva Corporum Regularium* with a dedication to the Emperor Maximilian. On opening the doors a whole panorama of polyhedra is revealed, carried out in intarsia using differently coloured woods.

BACKGROUND From Jamnitzer's *Perspectiva Corporum Regularium*, 1568.

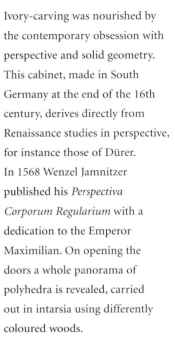

Further complicated demonstrations of perspective, with figures that could be followed by virtuoso craftsmen in ivory. These two woodcuts are from Lorenz Stoer's *Geometria*, Augsburg, 1576.

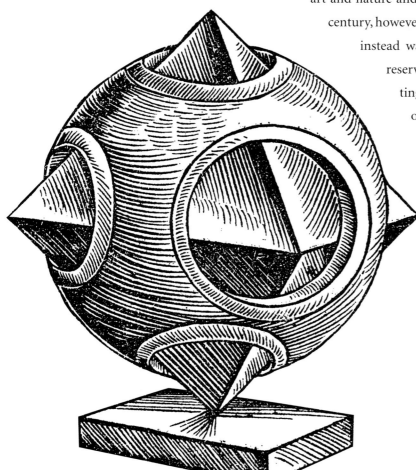

Natura stupet: 'nature is dumbfounded', wrote a Dutch still-life painter beside his signature:[16] marvels belong to a world beyond our own, invalidating all traditional notions of functionalism or usefulness. By virtue of this quality alone, by their ability to challenge the viewer's gaze and call into question accepted truths, marvels played a crucial part in the history of the cult of curiosities - a history which is itself, it could be argued, a chronicle of inverted values.[17] This positive force was advocated by Bacon, Hobbes and Descartes as a stimulus to enquiries into the very foundations of reality, the relationship between art and nature and the psychology of knowledge. By the late seventeenth century, however, it was no longer held in a respect verging on dread, but instead was viewed with the type of dismissive condescension reserved for naïve beliefs: 'Wonder was no longer reverential, tinged with awe and fear, but rather a low, bumptious form of pleasure.' Wonder was now nothing more than a form of blind, hallucinatory credulousness, and once again the cult of curiosities found itself relegated from the ranks of 'high' culture, and the fringes of scientific enquiry, to those of low culture, where charlatanism encountered aestheticism.

– Anselm Boethius de Boodt,
Gemmarum et Lapidum Historia, *1609*

*The Emperor [Rudolf II] is a lover of stones,
not simply in order that he may thereby
augment his dignity and majesty, but so
that in them the excellence of God may
be contemplated, the ineffable might of
Him who is seen to press the beauty
of the whole world into such exiguous
bodies and include in them the
powers of all other created things.*

– Sir Walter Raleigh, History of the World, *1614*

*For that infinite wisdom of GOD,
which hath distinguished his Angells by
degrees, which hath given greater and lesse
light and beautie to Heavenly bodies, which
hath made differences betweene beasts
and birds, created the Eagle and the flie,
the Cedar and the Shrub, and among stones
given the fairest tincture to the Rubie,
and the quickest light to the Diamond,
hath also ordained Kings, Dukes or Leaders
of the People, Magistrated, Judges and
other degrees among men.*

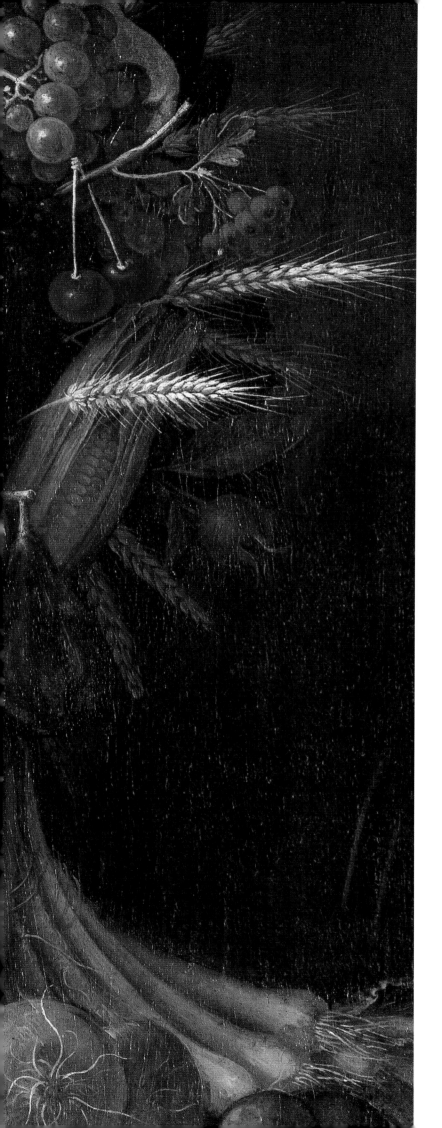

The Collector: 'senex puerilis'

The men who formed collections of curiosities could be members of the nobility able to buy anything, merchants whose collections were usually more specialized, and less wealthy intellectuals engrossed in some particular aspect of study.

It is possible to define the 'collector' as a psychological type, a man with a mania for completeness. By taking objects out of the flux of time he in a sense 'mastered' reality. Such an approach has been called 'childlike', though it was often combined with education and intellectual sophistication. Hence the description of the collector as '*senex puerilis*', the 'childish old man'.

The Emperor Rudolf II, prince of collectors, is treated at greater length later (pp. 164–73). This extraordinary portrait of him by his favourite painter Giuseppe Arcimbaldo shows him as Vertumnus, god of vegetation and the spring. Like all his works, it was intended to be read as an allegory.

Luft-Schloß
RAS
1
2
4

FERDINAND OF TYROL

PREVIOUS PAGE Schloss Ambras, near Innsbruck in Austria, was the seat of Ferdinand of Tyrol, Charles V's brother and Rudolf's uncle. He was in many ways the pioneer of imperial collecting, and his cabinet of curiosities became famous throughout Europe. Ferdinand was interested in natural wonders, works of art, bizarre monsters and human freaks.
This engraving by Merian (1648) is the earliest known view. Inset are portraits of Ferdinand and his wife Philippina Welser. The medieval castle occupies the hill. The *Kunstkammer* was one of the buildings in the lower courtyard.

RIGHT Sharks hang from the ceiling; in the foreground the horn of a deer impaled on a tree which has grown round it; on the wall is a life-size portrait of a giant, Giovanni Bona, with a dwarf. A French visitor in the 1690s, Charles Patin, wrote: 'At the end of one of the galleries I saw the representation of a giant and a dwarf, the living originals of which had sometime resided at Vienna. Indeed, this exorbitant inequality of stature between two men is a very strange thing.'

OPPOSITE The Spanish Hall of Ambras, commissioned by Ferdinand in 1570. This is one of the first Renaissance halls north of the Alps.

In the half-century leading up to the Thirty Years' War, the most celebrated cabinets of curiosities were to be found in the Germanic countries. Significantly, the majority of the collector-princes who vied with each other in the splendour of their collections at this period were closely related by blood. At the castle of Ambras near Innsbruck, Archduke Ferdinand II of Tyrol (1520–95), brother-in-law of Albrecht V of Bavaria, created what is considered today as the prototype of all *Wunderkammern*. Here a thousand objects, methodically classified, were laid out in some twenty large, glass-fronted cabinets, which were colour-coded according to the nature of the objects they contained: gold and silverware, precious stones, musical and scientific instruments, bronzes, items carved in wood,

porcelain, manuscripts, coins and medals and ethnographical curiosities. One room was devoted to historic weapons and Turkish trophies, another was a library and a third an *antiquarium*; the walls were hung with paintings, and a few rarities from the natural world, such as stuffed fish and sharks, were suspended from the ceiling. Though it was never made available to all sections of the public, the collection was intended from the outset to open to selected visitors.

Collectors are ruled by one law and one law only, that of the pursuit of the unique, the distinctive, the particular; they are driven, as Walter Benjamin observed, by a unique passion, that of 'protecting themselves against the abstract nature of the collective experience'.[18] Whatever is lost amid the blur of reality, whatever is circulated and exchanged, must first and foremost be removed from this flux, and preserved out of the way of use and exchange. There is nothing intellectual or of general import about this process; on the contrary, it is profoundly physical, even carnal. For the bibliophile, Benjamin continues, book-objects do not exist as such, but are merely *examples*, and the reality of each example may be experienced only through handling it, caressing it, fixing it in a particular spot in a particular part of a particular room. Similarly, the rarity of an object in the cult of curiosities is merely sketched in at first, in virtual time as it were, taking on its true meaning, or its reality, only once it is placed in this drawer or that, on this shelf or in that hidden recess of the cabinet. Even more clearly than the bibliophile, the collector of curiosities (who is also in part a bibliophile) makes use of 'the full gamut of infantile modes of acquisition, from holding it in his hands to the final culmination of giving it a name. A new perspective thus emerges from which to consider the aesthetics of the mount, sheath, casket or frame, of the *Kunstschrank*, of these spaces slotted one into another, as described above. All these now appear as so many steps or degrees in these modes of acquisition, or appropriation, which in Benjamin's view were so essential; modes which extend and amplify the passion for the acquisition of the dates, places, dimensions, origins and history specific to each object, and which in themselves offer all the data necessary for a catalogue.

For the collector, the acquisition of a piece 'is equivalent to its renaissance': its 'historical' identity, the half-real and half-imaginary qual-

ABOVE One of Ferdinand's bizarre musical instruments kept at Ambras.

OPPOSITE A majolica figure by Christoph Gandtner of a naked woman holding a cornucopia and sitting on a hedgehog symbolized (in the convoluted logic of Ferdinand's court) '*Furwitzigkeit*', or 'Presumptuousness'.

ity of the provenance and peregrinations that have left their mark on the piece, is overlaid with a new condition, or in substance a redefinition. Isolated, protected, regenerated, the object now escapes – through the collector's good offices and beneath his very eyes – the ineluctable processes of decay and death that had hitherto been its destiny. It is another instance of the recurring themes of life and death, and of the victory of the former over the latter. It was in this magnificent illusion, reinforced or acted out afresh by each new addition to the collection, that – Benjamin concluded – the 'childlike approach' of the collector lay: a prisoner of the very illusions that he exploited, he gloried in the eternal present of the cabinet of curiosities but at the same time was haunted by the transient nature of its collections.

This 'childlike approach' is indissociable from another, seemingly contradictory, element: borrowing the rhetorical figure of the *senex puerilis*, Benjamin describes it as inextricably intertwined with the 'aged approach', with all the latter's acute awareness of the temporal aspect and genealogy of their objects, whether natural or man-made. Relic, palimpsest of other eras and philosophies, piece of a puzzle or transitional plaything in a never-ending play of echoes and analogies, as we have seen, the object was in essence a manifestation of an age-old system of thought. Elias Ashmole, for instance, devoted many painstaking years to the creation of his miraculous 'ark' in the heart of Oxford, driven by the conviction that 'many secrets of nature had been divulged in remote antiquity and hence were available by careful scrutiny of ancient lore'.[19] This notion of an underlying continuity, of a regular and unceasing flow of coded information from the past to the present, was of central importance to Ashmole's 'mysterious and hierarchical' view of society. It was also an anachronistic and archaic approach that left him ill-prepared for the cataclysmic upheavals of the English Civil War, in which, scandalized by the 'licentious barbarisms of the late times', he not surprisingly espoused the royalist cause. As Michael Hunter explains, 'this sense of affront illustrates the feeling for cultural continuity which the monarchy came to symbolise so strongly for Ashmole, the reaction to the upheavals of the mid-seventeenth century'. The whole eclectic collection had been amassed by Ashmole in a magnificently serendipitous fashion.

OVERLEAF Portrait of a crippled dwarf made for Ferdinand, the head perfectly normal and dressed in the latest fashion, the body dreadfully stunted. Patin, who must have been typical of many visitors, was not attracted by such curiosities 'which I could never behold without a kind of horror'.

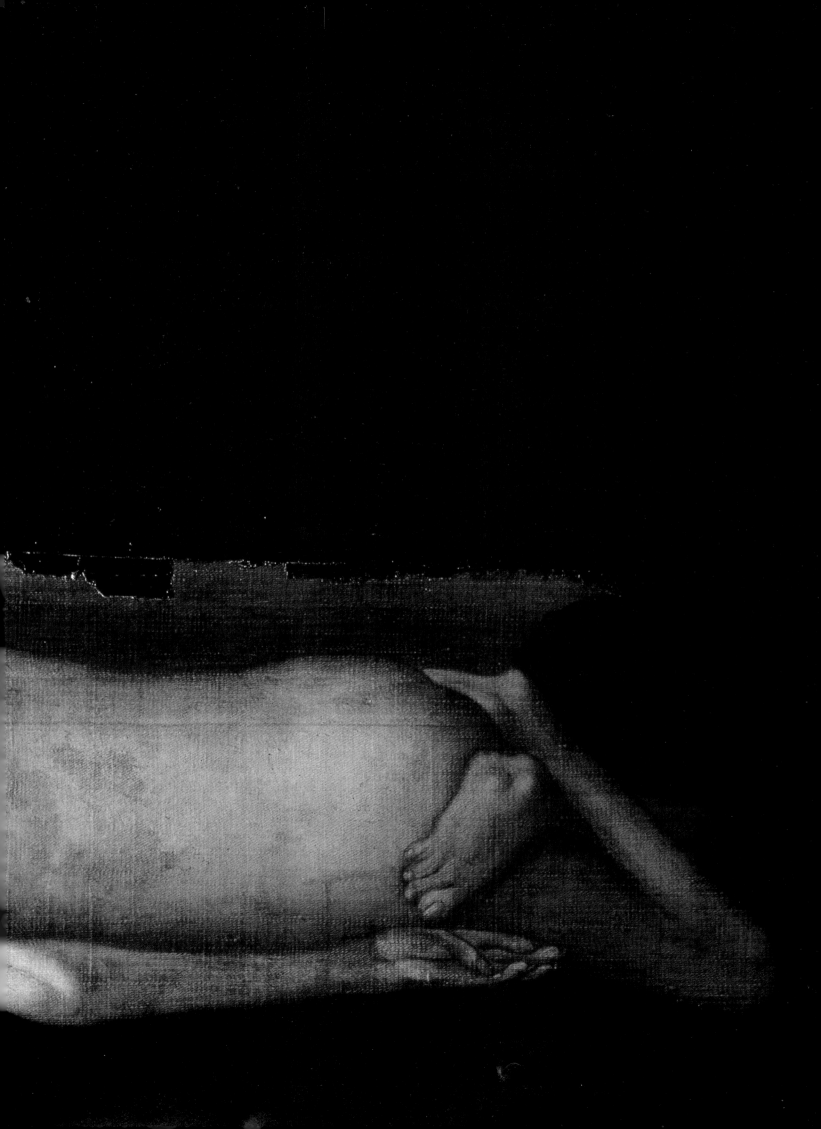

Near Ambras lived a family all of whom – men, women and children – were by some genetic abnormality copiously covered in hair. They were known as 'cat people' and Ferdinand delighted in having their portraits.

OPPOSITE 'I applied myself more particularly,' wrote Charles Patin, visiting Ambras about 1690, 'to the viewing of the portraiture of a certain *Hungarian* nobleman, which is not so much to be admired for the excellency of the draught, as for the prodigy which it represents, *viz*, a wound made with a lance in the eye, which penetrated into the substance of the brain, even to the hinder part of the head, and yet did not prove mortal. This is a secret of nature, that is altogether hid from us, and which confounds all our argumentations.'

OR. BAXI
G: NOB:

Tradescant Iun.t & his
epsa of Lambeth.

TRADESCANT AND ASHMOLE

In England the collection
of *naturalia* begins with John
Tradescant, who served as
gardener to various members
of the aristocracy culminating in
King Charles I. In the early 17th
century he travelled in Europe
and North Africa collecting plants
and bringing many new species
back to England. He established
a 'physic garden' at Lambeth,
in south London. Around 1625
he was joined by his son, also
called John, who travelled as
far as Virginia in the search
for specimens for the garden.
The Tradescants also collected
curiosities such as minerals
and shells and their whole
collection was known as
'the Ark'. Part of it forms the
setting for this double portrait
by Emanuel de Critz of the
younger Tradescant, on the left,
with a Lambeth neighbour,
the brewer Roger Friend.

John Tradescant the Younger left
'the Ark' to another English
collector, Elias Ashmole (right),
who in turn donated it to the
University of Oxford and it
became the nucleus of the
Ashmolean museum. It included
not just botanical specimens but
also shells, stuffed birds, works
of art (ivories and paintings),
artefacts from distant countries
(Buddhas and American Indian
costumes) and a hawking glove
of Henry VIII.

OPPOSITE John Tradescant
the Elder, set within a sort of
horticultured frame, attributed
to Cornelius de Neve.

But it was to serve as inspiration for the researches of 'true scholars'
such as Robert Hooke. Ultimately, the fact that – founded as it was on a
misguided premise – Ashmole's collection was both arbitrary and
pointless, served only to emphasize the essentially aesthetic nature of
the enterprise. There was a fundamentally *finished* quality about a collection of curiosities.

Although England had no tradition of dynastic collections of curiosities,
it nevertheless saw the burgeoning of one of the most impressive private
collections in Europe: that of the celebrated gardener and botanist John
Tradescant (1577–1638), who towards the end of his life founded a
museum of curiosities which he opened to the public. His son compiled
the catalogue in collaboration with Elias Ashmole (1617–92), who was to
inherit the collection, expanding it with items he had himself collected

S.r John   Tradescant Sen.r

PHILIPPE.LONG   LOUIS.HUTI

INNOCENT X

LE CHATEAU S.ᵗ GERMAIN PAR Mˢ LE DAVPHIN.

before offering it as a gift to the University of Oxford. The university lavished great expense on the construction of a special building to house it, which was inaugurated as the Ashmolean Museum in 1683. In France, meanwhile, an almost exact contemporary of John Tradescant the elder, Nicolas-Claude Peireisc (1580–1637), assembled among other rarities the finest collection of medals in the land, as well as distinguished collections of botanical and zoological items.

Lytton Strachey penned the following description of John Aubrey (1626–97), the antiquarian and unparalleled writer on the cult of curiosities whose collection only ever existed on paper: 'his mind moved in a circle of ideas which was rapidly becoming obsolete, and which, so long as our civilisation lasts, can never come into existence again'.[20] The 'maggotie-headed' Aubrey (his own description) shared the same world view as the insatiable John Evelyn (1620–1706), collector, traveller and historian of encyclopaedic scope, and the physician and accomplished essayist Sir Thomas Browne (1605–82). Owner of gardens, a library and a cabinet of curiosities that attracted numerous visitors, Browne was also one of the most sonorous writers of prose in the English language, with a fascination for the 'anomalies in the general Book of Nature' (*Pseudodoxia Epidemia*, or *Inquiries into Vulgar and Common Errors*, III, 15). But he too shared the conviction that the world was one great metaphor, an immense tissue of analogies. 'To thoughtful observers,' he noted in his *Christian Morals* (III, 10), 'the whole world is a phylactery, and everything we see is an item of the Wisdom, Power and Goodness of God.' Thus he was able to devote an entire treatise to the quincunx, in the belief that he had discovered in it a species of divine figure, found throughout nature in, for example, blood vessels, the art of gardens and insects' wings, not to mention the outer skin of pineapples. '*Natura nihil agit*,' he concluded in *Religio Medici* (I, 15): nature created everything with a purpose.

CLAUDE DU MOLINET

Father Claude Du Molinet was the librarian of the monastery of Ste Geneviève in Paris. Around 1675 he established there 'a cabinet of rare and curious pieces pertaining to study and what might serve literature, the sciences and above all history, natural, ancient and modern.' Its contents are known from a catalogue published after his death (he died in 1687), which illustrates the ensemble as well as the objects in it.

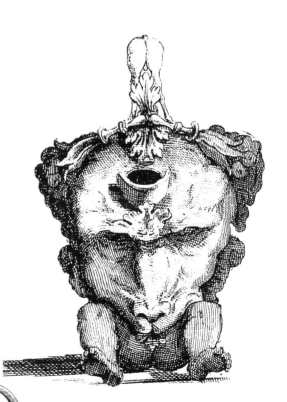

ANTIQVITATIS MEMORIAM FERDI

DA

VS EQ·BAYVL·ARRETII MAR·PETRIOLI SENATORQ·DE C

ALDROVANDI AND COSPI

Ferdinando Cospi (opposite) was an agent of the Medici family. As a young man towards the end of the 16th century he began collecting Roman and Etruscan antiquities and idols from Egypt and Mexico. But in 1605 he acquired the collection of Ulisse Aldrovandi, professor of natural history at the University of Bologna. As well as an extensive collection of plants, this contained thousands of illustrations prepared with the greatest accuracy. This monkey (above) is one.

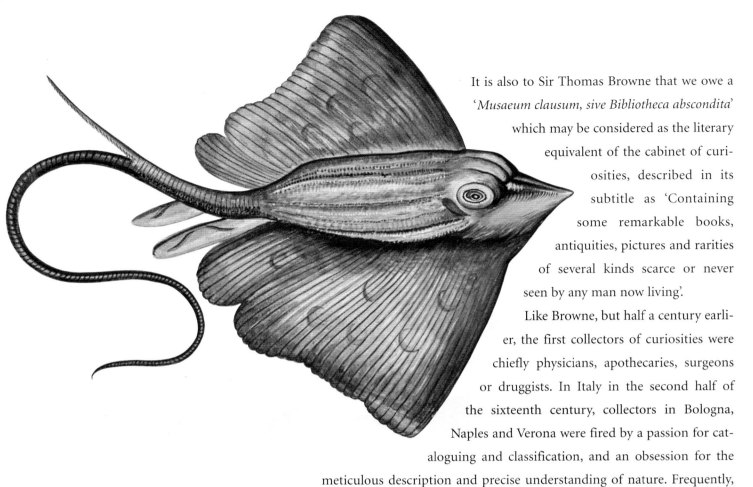

It is also to Sir Thomas Browne that we owe a 'Musaeum clausum, sive Bibliotheca abscondita' which may be considered as the literary equivalent of the cabinet of curiosities, described in its subtitle as 'Containing some remarkable books, antiquities, pictures and rarities of several kinds scarce or never seen by any man now living'.

Like Browne, but half a century earlier, the first collectors of curiosities were chiefly physicians, apothecaries, surgeons or druggists. In Italy in the second half of the sixteenth century, collectors in Bologna, Naples and Verona were fired by a passion for cataloguing and classification, and an obsession for the meticulous description and precise understanding of nature. Frequently, however, they appear (also like Browne) to have turned their backs on the realms of superstition and 'common error' only with reluctance, or to have embraced with eagerness the taste for the spectacular, the freakish and the bizarrely unique. And it is precisely this ambivalence – experienced or lived rather than consciously debated – between scientific ambition and aesthetic nostalgia, this essential ambiguity, this striving towards a discriminating approach while constantly lapsing into the world of the imagination, this interface (to use the most uncompromisingly modern term), which in our eyes constitutes the full value or feeling of these 'attempts at rigour' in the imagination. It is a vacillating journey of swings and counter-swings, most tellingly illustrated by a few brief lives of distinguished collectors.

At this period, the map of princely collections in Europe was shadowed by another network, quite as richly endowed and formed by the collections of scholars and connoisseurs from the merchant classes. Here again, the accepted dichotomy between northern and southern Europe conceals a reality that is both more complex and more subtle, an international language and a system of exchange that transcended national boundaries, as

One of Aldrovandi's volumes was devoted exclusively to fishes. He was not immune to the folkloric element in medieval bestiaries. Buffon said that he had 'a tendency towards credulity'. Of the sting-ray (*Pastinaca marina*) he wrote: 'they wound anyone who tries to catch them and inject a powerful poison. They love music, the dance and witty remarks.' BACKGROUND Woodcut from Aldrovandi's *Monstrorum historia*, 1642.

borne out once again by Quiccheberg's famous treatise of 1565. This brief practical guide to all those who wished to follow the princely example by embarking on a collection of curiosities also gave a detailed description of the distribution of private collections, both within Germany and without. Before publishing his work Quiccheberg had travelled extensively, most notably in Italy, where he visited most of the great private collections of international influence. An entire chapter of his treatise – entitled *Exempla ad lectorem* – was devoted to the private collections of scholars and connoisseurs, many of whom were also his friends.

Foremost among these distinguished figures, both in chronology and in the quality of his collections, was the Italian Ulisse Aldrovandi (1522–1605). He founded a 'museum' in Bologna which was freely accessible to scholars, a paradigm of the encyclopaedic cabinet conceived as an instrument of observation and classification, as created by most of the great collectors of the sixteenth century, irrespective of nationality. Though these are too numerous to list here in full, some of the earliest examples in Italy were the collections of Antonio Giganti (1535–98), linked organically to a library and classified according to a symmetrical system alternating works of art with works of nature; the Vatican's *Metalloteca*, created by the botanist Michele Mercati (1541–93); the collection of the apothecary Francesco Calzolari (1521–1600) in Verona; and the extremely wide-ranging museum founded in Naples by another apothecary, Ferrante Imperato (1550–1615). The last two both formed a functional combination of cabinet of curiosities and strictly scientific laboratory.

Professor of philosophy and natural history at the university of Bologna, as well as director of the town's botanical museum, Aldrovandi is undoubtedly one of the most familiar figures in the history of the cult of curiosities. Like Calzolari and Imperato, he was a *homo novus* or new man, was not a member of the aristocracy, did not enjoy any private patronage, possessed a scientific education and eschewed the passions for symbolism and the occult that inspired the iconographic programme of the *studiolos* of the Medicis. Collect, observe, compare: these were Aldrovandi's guiding principles.

The porcupine fish (*orbis*) from Aldrovandi. Apart from his natural history interests, Aldrovandi seriously studied palaeography, law, logic, philosophy, medicine, mathematics, geometry, astronomy and the use of the astrolabe. This was virtually the last time when a man could, in Bacon's words, 'take all knowledge for his province'.

He conceived his cabinet of curiosities as a collection of samples, as exhaustive and encyclopaedic as possible, of 'cose sotterranee, et conchilij et Ostraceî', each item performing the function, as Olmi has observed,[21] of an index card in a universal catalogue. The two principal display cupboards in his cabinet together contained no fewer than 4,554 drawers. Justly proud of this extravagant system of classification, he dwelt at length on its unparalleled virtues in a letter to Francesco de' Medici in 1577, drawing particular attention to the device by which the cassetti in the display cupboards opened to reveal smaller cassettini concealed within them.[22]

Driven by his desire to captivate and impress, he was not unaware of the importance of visitors, who rapidly elevated his cabinet to the ranks of one of Bologna's most popular attractions, and produced a Catalogus virorum qui visitarunt Musaeum nostrum, in which he categorized his visitors according to their geographical origins and social standing ('secundum ordinem dignitatem, studiorum et professionum').

Obsessive and indefatigable, he would write notes on scraps of paper and place them in bags, alphabetically arranged, before doggedly re-ordering them once again and gluing them on to sheets. At his death, he left 360 manuscript volumes, some of which remain unpublished to this day.

Possessed by this vaulting ambition to create an inventory of the world, Aldrovandi was bound before long to come up against the impossibility of obtaining a specimen of every plant and animal that he required. If he could not have them in the flesh, then he would have images of them: by the time of his death he had duly amassed nearly eight thousand panels bearing representations in tempera of the exotic or rare objects from nature of which he had been unable to obtain specimens. And these were in addition to the eleven thousand beasts, plants and minerals in his collection, and the seven thousand pressed plants that he amassed and glued into fifteen volumes. In Aldrovandi's world, the art of portraiture was totally subordinate to the desire to document, and this presupposed a means of transmission or communication.

Ulisse Aldrovandi at the age of seventy-eight. Aldrovandi was a man with an irresistible passion for accumulating and recording information. When he went to Rome as a young man he made a list of all the ancient statues in the city and where they were. When he returned to take up a university post in Bologna, he applied the same energy and industry to the natural world. 'Nothing is sweeter than to know all things,' he said.

Aldrovandi's cabinet thus found its logical extension in Aldrovandi's books. He devoted the greater part of his life to compiling an interminable encyclopaedia, three volumes of which were printed during his lifetime, with a further ten appearing posthumously. On his death he also left a *Pandechion Epistemonicon* in eighty-three manuscript volumes, with wood engravings so numerous that they filled no fewer than fourteen of the cabinets in his museum. His *Monstrorum Historia*, meanwhile, published in 1642 by one of his students, was a compendium of every known instance of animal or human monstrosity, which offered a clear demonstration of the way in which the scientific aspect of his ventures, with its underlying relativist hypothesis of the influence of the historical and geographical context on social conditioning,[23] tipped over into the realm of myth and fable. In its pages, the image of a '*pater annorum quadraginta et filius annorum viginti toto corpore pilosi*', depicting two celebrated cases of hirsutism, is juxtaposed with fantastical representations of races described by Pliny, alongside reproductions of ancient treatises.[24] Both demonstrate the degree to which, in his unquenchable thirst for knowledge, Aldrovandi was susceptible to 'the love of rarity, the typically mannerist taste for the bizarre and unusual objects'.[25]

In 1603, Aldrovandi endowed his collection to the city of Bologna. After his death, in 1617, it was transferred to the Palazzo Pubblico, and in 1657 it was combined with the collection of Marchese Ferdinando Cospi; a joint catalogue was published by Lorenzo Legati eighteen years later (*Museo Cospiano Annesso a quello del famoso Ulisse Aldrovandi*, Bologna, 1667). The engraving on the frontispiece, showing the cabinet in its final incarnation, invites commentaries on numerous different levels: beneath the unblinking gaze of Dante, every surface of the room, from walls to ceiling and down to the last square centimetre, is pressed into service as display space. The dozen or so display cabinets that are visible are crammed brimful of objects and all obey one rule exclusively: that of symmetry, the only law capable of imposing a veneer of order on a state of affairs that was actually a mockery of it, for here a methodical appearance offered all the force and substance of orderliness. The upper part of the image thus compares and reveals affinities between a seemingly eclectic welter of objects, including quantities of stuffed diodons (an exotic fish) jostling with improbable species of flying fish, animals resembling hybrids between eagles and porpoises, a creature

By 1570 Aldrovandi had collected 7,000 specimens of dried plants, as well as birds, animals and fishes. In addition he employed a team of artists to make coloured drawings of everything in the collection, which he gathered into thirteen large folio volumes.

BACKGROUND Engravings from *Museo Cospiano*, 1677.

The Red heron (*Ardea stellaria*)
and Guenon monkey
(*Cercopithecus barbiger*).
The monkey, said Aldrovandi,
was sent to a wine shop in the
West Indies with a flask in one
hand and money in the other
and fetched wine for his master.
Of the heron: 'the neck is very
thin and no less than a foot-
and-a-half long.'

Ardea stellaris ruffa, uel
Rusbÿ circa Verbanum lacum.

Simia Barbara.

claimed to be a mermaid, and other unidentifiable beasts with the hind legs of mammals and the tails of reptiles.

In the upper right-hand corner of the engraving, an elegant figure resembling a shadow puppeteer – perhaps Cospi himself? – proudly presents his theatre of the world. Beside him stands the dwarf who (we are told) acted as guide to this realm of curiosities, an ambivalent figure who seems as if possessed by this liminal space he inhabits, presiding over a world of objects in which he himself is in the end just another exhibit.

Inspired more by the apothecary's shop than the *studiolo*, these Italian collections were in many respects similar to the cabinets being created at the same time in the countries of northern Europe. One such collection was that assembled by the Basle naturalist Conrad Gesner (1516–65), friend and correspondent of Quiccheberg, which is often cited as an exemplar in its classification of the animal kingdom; others were those created by two other friends of the Belgian scholar, the botanist Leonhard Fuchs (1501–66) and the theologian, philosopher and mineralogist Georg Agricola (1494–1555). Yet another was the collection of ethnography and natural history amassed by the physician Bernhard Paludanus (1550–1633), originally of Enkhuizen in the Low Countries, which in the mid-seventeenth century was bought by the Duke of Gottorf to form the nucleus of the ducal *Kunstkammer*. And finally, in this by no means exhaustive list, comes the celebrated cabinet of Ole Worm (1588–1654), professor of medicine in Copenhagen, traveller, archaeologist and linguist, whose natural history collection was enriched by items of ethnographic interest and antiquities of Scandinavian and oriental origin, as well as Greek and Roman artefacts and works of art.

The same ambivalence is found in the earliest surviving image of a private museum, a more southerly equivalent of the collections of Aldrovandi in Bologna and Francesco Calzolari in Verona. The engraving on the frontispiece of the *Historia naturale di Ferrante Imperato napolitano libri XXVIII, nella quale ordinatamente si tratta della diversa condition di miniere e piere,con alcune storie di piante et animale sinora non date in luce*, published in Naples in 1599, depicts a more orderly but no less crowded interior than that of Aldrovandi's cabinet. In this instance, the collection is laid out in similarly symmetrical fashion around its imposing centrepiece: an enormous crocodile suspended from the ceiling. Meanwhile, above

OPPOSITE '*Torre d'avorio*', ivory tower, a piece of virtuoso carving of the sort cultivated by Settala (p. 158).

three other stuffed birds in the right-hand corner, closer inspection reveals what appears to be a pelican pecking at its breast:[26] a reference to the myth that the bird restored its offspring to life with its own blood, a trait that was adopted as a stock image for Christ's redemption of man.

The naturalist and apothecary Imperato (1550–1625) declared none the less, and no doubt with complete sincerity, 'My Theatre of Nature consists only of objects from nature, such as plants, minerals and animals'. By virtue of this principle, he counted among his most prized possessions a bezoar reputed to have saved the life of a physician during an outbreak of plague, and he was a fervent believer in the healing powers of stones (a subject to which his son devoted a treatise, *De fossilibus opusculum*, in 1610): 'An amethyst, for example, when worn on the navel, frees a person of intoxication. Sapphire cleanses the eyes and extinguishes lust. Crystal restrains poisonous draughts, while nephrite guards against gravel in the kidneys and stomaches. A compound of topaz, sappyre, sardonyx, hyacinth, and granite is an excellent antidote to poisons; wearing jasper, on the other hand, prevents hemeorreage and menses and facilitates the natural virtues of the stomach.'[27]

Credulous though he may have been, Imperato should nevertheless be given due credit for debunking a number of ill-founded beliefs, demonstrating for example that toadstone did not derive from toads, but presented some similarities to toadstools. And the apparent chaos of his cabinet of curiosities corresponded in his conception to the transitional distribution of the elements (which also provided the structure for his *Natural History*): salts, minerals, metals, earth, water, air and fire.

The publication of the *Natural History* and its frontispiece in 1599 played a not insignificant part in spreading the collection's fame, and it rapidly became a choice attraction for intellectuals of the period, including the scholar Federico Cesi, the German physician Johann Faber and the celebrated Cassiano del Pozzo, who subsequently exchanged letters. Only the persistent and doubtless well-founded rumours that the true author of the fifty-eight volumes of the *Natural History* was not in fact Imperato but was much more likely to be one Nicola Antonio Stigliola (1546–1623) were to cast a shadow over the reputations of Imperato father and son. Leaping to their defence, Federico Cesi persisted in believing that father and son were '*miracoli di natura, et molto più di quello che si dice*'.[28]

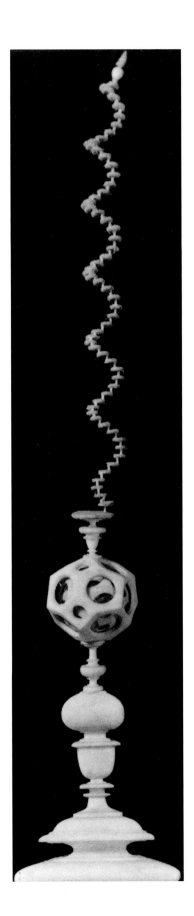

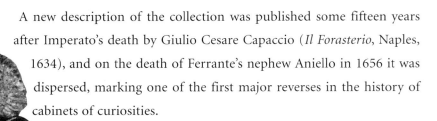

A new description of the collection was published some fifteen years after Imperato's death by Giulio Cesare Capaccio (*Il Forasterio*, Naples, 1634), and on the death of Ferrante's nephew Aniello in 1656 it was dispersed, marking one of the first major reverses in the history of cabinets of curiosities.

Historians frequently cite the cabinet of curiosities established by Francesco Calzolari (*c.* 1521–*c.* 1606) in Verona as the northern counterpart of Imperato's collection. Also an apothecary by profession, Calzolari considered his private museum as a sort of laboratory and seminar room, to be used for practical work, encounters and discussions between students, and operating in a close and fruitful relationship with his dispensary. This was the view reflected in the first catalogue, published in 1584 (Giovanni Battista Oliva, *De Reconditis, et praecipuis collectaneis ab honestissimo et sollertissimo Francesco Calceolario Veronensi in museo adservatis*). A second catalogue, published some fifteen years after Calzolari's death, marked an increasing propensity towards the bizarre. Its authors, Benedetto Ceruto and Andrea Chiocco (*Musaeum Franc. Calceolari*, Verona, 1622), dwelt at length on the strange or magical properties of the objects in the collection: here there was no doubt that toadstone emanated from the skulls of toads; that a true fragment of a unicorn's horn possessed healing powers; or that a curious plant by the poetic name of *Lunaria* displayed 'magnet-like properties that, according to lore, have the power to extract nails from the hoofs of horses grazing on mountain fields'.[29]

It was this second catalogue that contained the engraving of Calzolari's cabinet of curiosities that is familiar to us today: influenced, as has been observed, by Imperato's. The focal point of the image is provided by a display cabinet with a broken pediment containing thirty-two niches; a pair of obelisks and another of carved figures make discreet references to analogies and correspondences, while on the shelves, vases and canopic jars offer a decorative counterpoint to a collection of shells. More overtly even than in Imperato's cabinet, the internal architecture of the room, the design of the *arredi* or furnishings, the studied elegance and the emphatic decorative scheme all indicate a desire to impose a system or order on a disparate world: the intelligible was here a structure grafted on to the living flesh.

A similar obsession with symmetry was to be found in the cabinet of curiosities created by Antonio Giganti (1535–98) in Bologna.[30] This cabinet belonged to 'the cultural strand of ecclesiastical humanism in the Italian Renaissance' at the time of the Council of Trent, however, and so represented the complementary obverse of collections that were purely scientific in intent. 'Two kinds of symmetry', observed Minelli, 'can be detected amongst the exhibits on the walls of the studio: the first, concerning the display of individual items, may be termed "alternate microsymmetry", in which items of similar appearance are never displayed next to one another, but invariably alternate with other or similar objects; the second system, which we may call "repeating macrosymmetry", involved the arrangement of groups of items on a thematic basis.' Close scrutiny of the engraving of the Calzolari collection would certainly reveal the same thematic and structural principles at work, but here fulfilling different functions. The guiding principle of the collection assembled by Giganti, who was secretary to two prominent members of the clergy, was not so much scientific 'specialization' as a general exaltation of creation in all its forms, with the purpose of emphasizing the hidden unity of the universe. But over and above their differing objectives, these three collectors were united by 'a strong desire to fill every space – making no distinction between *naturalia* and *artificialia* – and to achieve an effect of harmonious symmetry'.[31]

The penchant for the spectacular that was inherent in the creation of any cabinet of curiosities was to become progressively more marked, with objets d'art and bizarre or esoteric items occupying an increasingly dominant place. This development may be explained at least in part by the growing presence in everyday life of exotic objects, which were now imported from the colonies in ever-increasing numbers.[32] Imperceptibly, the cabinet of curiosities opened up the intimate space of the private galleries in which medals were displayed alongside paintings and sculptures, claiming for its collections the status of fully-fledged 'objets d'art'. As a new generation of collectors flourished in the first half of the seventeenth century, so – in Olmi's view – the emphasis shifted to the specifically aesthetic quality of the objects, and to a quest for the type of effects befitting the age of the Baroque.

Still in Italy, a portrait of Manfredo Settala, who lived in Milan between 1600 and 1680, offers a perfect example of this

In the course of the 18th century Manfredo Settala's collection (see next page) was acquired by the Bibliotecca Ambrosiona, Milan, where it still is. It included these two shell masks.

MANFREDO SETTALA

Settala, born in 1600 and dying in 1680, was one of the most notable private collectors of the 17th century. His cabinet included natural objects, works of craftsmanship and a number of reliquaries classified not by the saints whose relics they contained but by the materials they were made of. He was once called to the monastery of S. Maria delle Grazie where one of the monks had been mysteriously killed in the cloister by a stone falling from the sky. This would formerly have been explained as a supernatural intervention, but Settala correctly diagnosed it as a thunderbolt (i.e. a meteorite) before calmly appropriating the evidence for his collection. He was adept at turned ivory, which he is shown holding (above), and astronomical instruments, such as the celestial sphere (opposite).

phenomenon: his features composed in an expression of melancholy, he delicately proffers a turned ivory piece that is a virtuoso exercise in ingenuity and skill, thus offering the viewer the visual equivalent of a rhetorical flourish, as impressive as it is ultimately futile. Himself a builder of scientific and mechanical instruments, Settala viewed microscopes, telescopes, compasses and other complex horological mechanisms not so much as 'working instruments but as precious objects, to be appreciated more from an aesthetic than a practical point of view'.[33] Milan at this period was moreover considered one of the principal centres for the production of minutely detailed objects in wood, gold, ivory and crystal, technical *tour de forces* requiring the utmost skill.

Thanks to his remarkable cabinet, Settala rapidly became far more than merely a local celebrity. Having inherited his father's collection, he set about enriching every aspect of it, attracting ever-growing numbers of visitors of a broad range of nationalities and social classes. Claiming in his turn that his cabinet represented an image of the world, and in his own fashion picking up where Aldrovandi left off, he commissioned nearly three hundred drawings of objects in his collection from numerous artists, which he subsequently published in seven volumes, arranged by subject matter and with accompanying notes.[34] The first catalogue of Settala's collection, drawn up by Paolo Maria Terzago, was published in 1664. While still doggedly crammed to the point of overflowing with a plethora of objects, the space is more open than the cocoon-like cabinets of earlier collectors. The box of what might be termed the *camera curiosa*, with one side removed, had now given way to a large room flanked by a pair of galleries defined by a series of display cabinets, each with six doors. We know that Settala's collections filled four of the rooms of his residence, Via Pantano, with skeletons and automata, pressed plants and mineral samples, paintings and archaeological finds, weapons and clocks and a great deal more.[35] The dramatic nature of the galleries' architecture, meanwhile, seemed already to be in thrall to the laws of Baroque theatricality. So distinguished was Settala's reputation by the time of his death in 1680, that his fellow citizens determined to bury him with the greatest pomp and ceremony: accordingly, a funeral cortege consisting of the most eccentric and outlandish pieces in his collection was headed by his own mortal remains, now also an empty relic of reality.

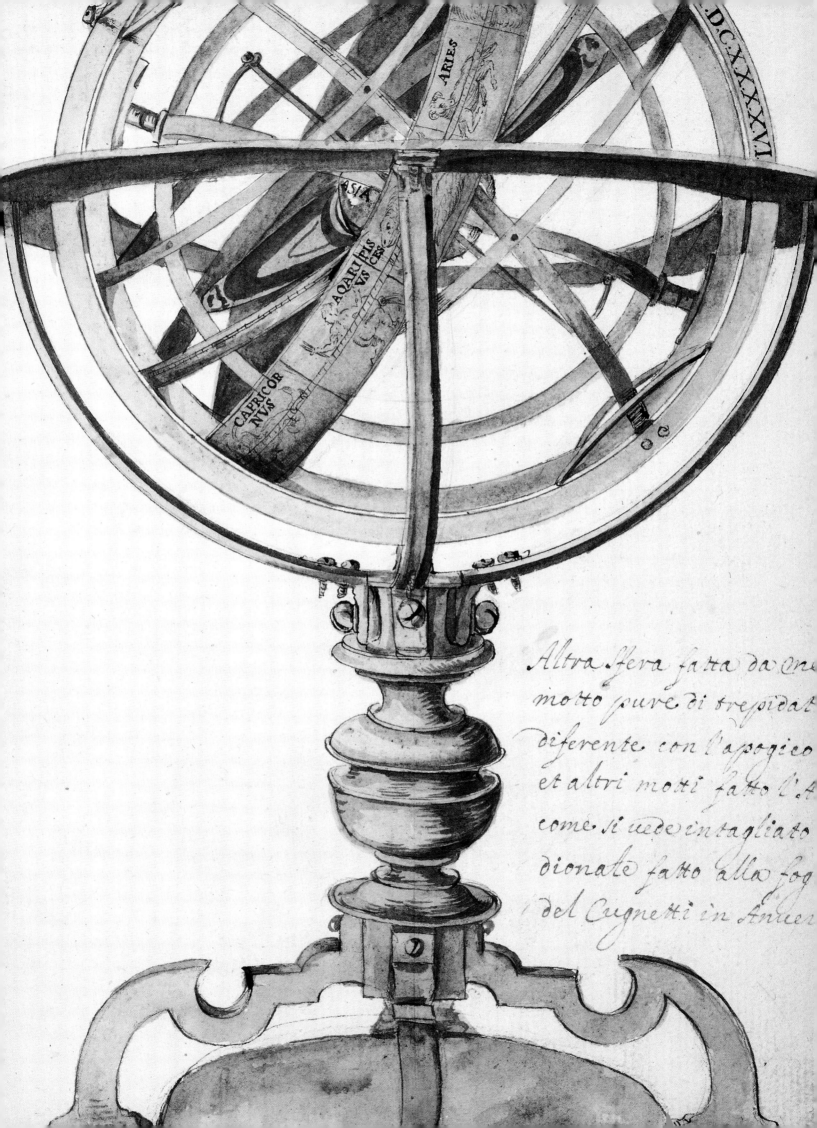

.D.C.XXXXVI.

ARIES

ASIA

AQARIPIS
VS CES

CAPRICOR
NVS

Altra sfera fatta da one
motto pure di trepidat
diferente con l'apogico
et altri moti fatto l'A
come si vede intagliato
dionate fatto alla fog
del Cignetti in Anuer

AN. M.DC.LXIV. IHS P. ATHANASIUS KIRCHERUS FULDENSIS E SOCIETATE IESU

The most admired polymath of southern Europe was Athanasius Kircher (1602–84), the 'dinosaur of the Baroque', who was German by birth but lived and worked in Italy. In Rome, he became professor of languages and mathematics at the Jesuit College. Rather vaguely described in 1633 by Nicolas Peiresc as 'a certain Jesuit priest by the name of Athanasius Kircher', within thirty years he had become one of the outstanding figures of Rome in the Baroque era, with a museum described as '*celeberrimum*'. The first catalogue devoted to his collections was published in 1678. An immensely prolific author, he was reputed to have 'produced more books than the Trojan horse did soldiers'[36], publishing in his lifetime no fewer than thirty-five volumes 'treating such subjects as magnetism, ancient hieroglyphics, astronomy, music, the hidden mysteries of numbers, the subterranean world, and the history of the Flood'.

Kircher's collections were substantially indebted to the rules and financial support of the Jesuits, as well as including 'finds' contributed by them. While traditional categories – fragments from antiquity, objects from the natural world and zoological items – were well represented, Kircher's collections also featured a wealth of Chinese, Japanese, Indian, African and native American pieces, sent back to Rome by missionary expeditions. Swelled by this unique source of exotica, as well as from bequests of collections of antiquities, in 1651 the museum was transferred from a single room adjacent to the library to the gallery depicted on the frontispiece of the volume published in 1678.

Ancient Egypt was one of Kircher's favoured fields of study, and the subject to which he devoted one of his most celebrated treatises (*Lingua Aegyptiaca Restituta*, 1643). Continuing his attempts to decode the language of the hieroglyphs, he followed this a decade later with his *magnum opus*, an encylcopaedic work on all things Egyptian which he called his *Oedipus Aegyptiacus* (1652–4). To his visitors, including the deferential John Evelyn, he appeared to be invested with a mysterious power that conferred upon him a

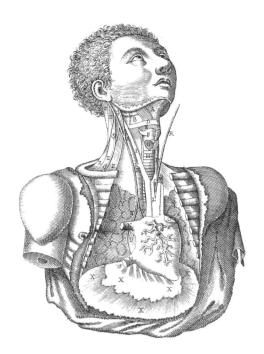

ATHANASIUS KIRCHER

Kircher, born in Germany but spending most of his life as a Jesuit in Rome, was one of the most famous polymaths of his age. John Evelyn visited him in 1644: 'Father Kircher (professor of mathematics and the oriental tongues) showed us many singular courtesies, and finally his own study, where, with Dutch patience, he showed us his perpetual motions, catoptrics, magnetical experiments, models, and a thousand other crotchets and devices.' Kircher's proudest achievement – or so he (wrongly) thought – was to have deciphered Egyptian hieroglyphics. Egyptian antiquities loom large in the engraving of his museum (opposite). ON THIS PAGE Engravings from his *Physiologia Kircheriana*, 1680, and *Musurgia universalis*, 1650.

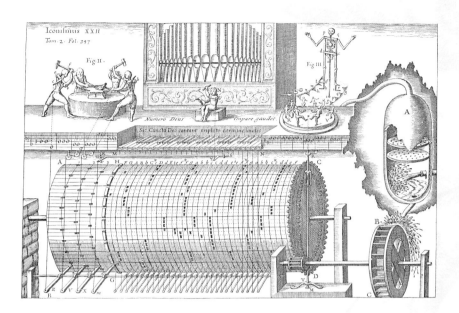

familiarity – whether real or supposed – with the lore and learning of ancient civilizations, and an ability to solve age-old secrets and riddles the keys to which had long been lost.[37]

Kircher was also exceptional in the way in which he displayed his collections, complementing his *naturalia* and relics with inventions and reconstructions, operated by himself, of a variety of wonders. These included the Delphic oracle, a sunflower clock and a variety of optical and visual illusions (many of which were re-created for a retrospective exhibition in Rome in 2000). Ever in search of spectacular effects, he installed a long acoustic tube, carefully concealed, between the gallery and his private chamber, so that his astonished visitors found themselves greeted by the sound of his disembodied voice.

While claiming for himself the utmost scientific rigour, Kircher was concerned above all to establish the connections that he was convinced existed between the hermetic systems of thought of antiquity and those of the Christian church. While the engraving of 1678 clearly depicts the gallery, it distorts its proportions, and transforms it into 'an extension of the cosmos, a microcosm linked directly to the macrocosm'.[38] Though he took note of the results of his observations and experiments, for the most part Kircher failed to draw accurate conclusions from them, enthralled as he was by his collections of facts, and not distinguishing between scientific knowledge and hermetic interpretation. As a result, he has attracted criticism for the 'dubious worth' of his learning and the 'backwardness of his thinking'.[39]

Among Kircher's interests was music, and his treatise *Musurgia Universalis* (1650), in which he discusses both the old polyphonic style and the new language of Baroque and of opera, is still read today. He wrote music himself, and was the first to put forward the theory that music is an expression of the emotions. At the pope's request, he designed a mechanical organ (mechanics being another of his talents). On the principle of the barrel-organ, a rotating drum (powered by water, shown on the right in each drawing), activates the keys and pipes, and at the same time moves various automata at the top, including a bird that flaps its wings. BACKGROUND engraving from *Physiologia Kircheriana*, 1680.

RVDOLPH. I
ROM. IMP. A
CHID. AVST
NAT. VIENA
MENSE IV
18. ANTE
POST M

'The world is to me but a dreame, or mockshow,' declared Sir Thomas Browne in *Religio Medici* (I, 41), and wee all therein but Pantalones, and Anticks to my severer contemplation': paradoxically, this passion for objects, for the tangible and material, tended to induce a sense of loss of reality, a heightened awareness of the largely fugitive, illusory nature of appearance and reality. The world of the cult of curiosities was imbued with melancholy. Browne himself, like Aubrey and also like Francesco de' Medici before both of them, was 'saturnine' of temperament and prey to 'leaden' humours, meditative by nature and obsessed with the passage of time and the pursuit – as futile as it was unending – of knowledge. The life of the most famous of all collectors of curiosities, Rudolf II of Habsburg (1552–1612), was punctuated and at times governed by the ineluctable emergence of his 'temperament'.

RUDOLF II

The Emperor Rudolf II was the greatest collector of them all. Nothing was outside the scope of his interests, and his resources were virtually limitless. OPPOSITE his portrait in wax, 1606, by Wenzel Maller.

ABOVE head of a 'Nile horse' (hippopotamus?) in Rudolf's collection.

LEFT beetle from Hofnägel's *Archetypa*, 1592.

In 1574, at the age of twenty-seven, he was laid low by one of his first episodes of depression, and four years later he succumbed to an even more debilitating attack which drove him to leave Vienna for the reputedly more favourable climate of Prague. Far from losing his taste for affairs of state, however, he continued to play his part fully until 1600, shielding himself behind elaborate court ceremonials and numerous displays, festivals, carnivals and tournaments directed by the most celebrated artists of the time, including Arcimboldo. But another episode of depression in 1600 brought with it a more urgent need to withdraw from the world, while also increasing his hunger for works of art of every kind. But these defences were to prove too fragile, and the latter part of his life was overshadowed by the scheming of his entourage, and particularly of his brother Matthias, to depose him. Having successfully resisted these machiavellian manoeuvres, despite being plunged into another even more profound attack of melancholy in 1605, a few years later he agreed to renounce his belief in his absolute power. By the time of his death in 1612, after continuing plots to usurp him, he had conceded a degree of autonomy to a certain number of his subjects.

An ambivalent attitude to power, withdrawal from the world, seeking refuge in art, an insatiable thirst for new acquisitions, a quest for the rare and bizarre: all of these characteristics combine to make Rudolf II the quintessential example of the breed of collector that we have attempted to describe in these pages. With his 'dogged adherence to medieval ways of thought',[40] he was clearly susceptible to the pervasive nostalgia and passion for the archaic typical of so many collectors. In his view the world consisted of finite groups or series, of sets that had to be completed, whether natural or artistic (such as the paintings of Correggio's *Loves of the Gods* cycle, which he collected incessantly). Beyond the unconstrained eclecticism of his acquisitions, there emerged a quest for fundamental unity, woven from analogies, correspondences and echoes.

Rudolf took delight in the drawings of plants and animals by a favourite artist Joris Hofnaegel, whom he commissioned to decorate some of his manuscripts, even when the subjects were quite irrelevant. Many were accurately observed, others allegorical, and some wholly fantastic, such as the carnations growing out of a globe that rests on the back of a lobster.

– *Samuel Quiccheberg, c. 1560*

A person of moderate fortune will thus, through the nature of the place where he finds himself and through his intentions and interests, most profitably accumulate different kinds of seeds, or metals, or small creatures, or old coins, or a collection of pictures, all without incurring great costs. The impression is not to be given that there is a lack of space, either broad or narrow, for all this to be stored. There is much that can be rolled up or folded and stowed away in slim cabinets, small cupboards or boxes, but for which, when they are otherwise stretched out over the broadest walls or exhibited on the widest tables or on measured display stands, there would scarcely be room enough. But here, in addition to these cupboards, chests, wall cabinets, tables and display stands, one must also call to mind that for these practical purposes storage magazines may be of great use, as well as portable boxes with square compartments, and small cupboards with folding doors, and likewise books with folding covers, and finally stacked chests containing sundry works of art and prominently labelled.

The Miseroni family of Milan
were recognized as the most
skilled goldsmiths of their age.
The great courts of Europe vied
for their services. Most expert
of all was Gasparo Miseroni, who
worked for both the Medici and
the Habsburgs. For the Emperor
Maximilian II, around 1570,
he made a fantastic vase of
chrysoprase (opposite), whose
handles are harpies of enamelled
gold enriched with pearls and
rubies. LEFT detail of a *tazza* with
stirrup-shaped handles in lapis
lazuli, mounted on gold lion
masks, another work of Gasparo
Miseroni. Both these objects
found their way into Rudolf II's
Kunstkammer.

Finally and most significantly, no aspect of his character (and not least his desire to embrace the diversity of creation while fleeing the real world) was untouched by melancholy: indeed it was the justification of the collections he envisaged.

Naturally the psychology of the collector offers rich material for applied psychoanalysis, and interpretations on this level are not lacking: a defence mechanism against anguish and the experience of loss, a bulwark against the fear of abandonment and the dread of being alone and defenceless, 'such behaviour has all the hallmarks of typical anal-obsessive character traits. In the emperor's case, they seem to have been an attempt to ward off feelings of depression, a condition that is not too unusual among many collectors [...]. The objects acquired (in Rudolf's case, it was almost irrelevant what they were – just anything that would arouse his curiosity) work like a protecting or reassuring device, as though they incorporated some form of magic.'[41]

Like Albrecht of Bavaria, Rudolf employed agents to scour the length and breadth of Europe for suitably remarkable items, and in addition he surrounded himself with artists and craftsmen, scholars and technicians whose brief was to create singular and extraordinary pieces. The collection was distinguished particularly by its eight hundred paintings of exceptional quality. It was methodically arranged in three great chambers of the Prague residence (the *vordere Kunstkammer*), which were considered as the antechamber to the *Kunstkammer* proper. The latter was principally devoted to *naturalia* (covering the four great realms of natural history, zoology, botany and mineralogy), *scientifica* (clocks and watches, astronomical instruments, terrestrial and celestial globes and compasses), *artificialia* (weapons, textiles, coins and medals from every continent, prints, precious furniture and above all items of craftsmanship in the broadest sense of the term, fashioned from organic and inorganic materials including ivory, amber, horn, ostrich eggs, metals and precious stones), and lastly a library. The three galleries that served as an introduction to the *Kunstkammer* contained displays of the same types of object, with the addition of works from antiquity: small bronzes, busts, statues, cameos and gems.

Taken as a whole, the collection of works of art and curiosities thus put together by Rudolf II is considered as one of the most discriminating of its time. And although in its sheer scale it cannot be compared with

Among Rudolf's passions was clocks. This photograph (opposite) shows the usually hidden workings inside an extraordinary clock in the form of a ship. Rudolf is represented sitting on a throne while the other six German electors process round him on the hour. It was made in Augsburg about 1580 by Hans Schottheim.

BACKGROUND engravings from L. E. Bergeron, *Manuel du turneur*, 1792.

Three precious examples of the goldsmith's art at the court of Rudolf II.

OPPOSITE A rhinoceros-horn cup by Nikolaus Pfaff (1611). The two horns, believed to be from a dragon, are actually the tusks of a warthog.

LEFT Details from a silver-gilt ewer by Nikolaus Schmidt, late 16th-century, inlaid with pearls and mother-of-pearl.

ABOVE Bezoar cup and ewer by Jan Vermeyer, c. 1600. Bezoar was a stone which when hollowed out into a cup was believed to render poisons harmless.

collections in Latin countries, it nevertheless shares a common aim with some of their number: not merely to amass a collection of objects, but also to manipulate reality, to experiment and invent. In this respect, the active presence of craftsmen and the existence of workshops within the very confines of Rudolf's court did not differ so very much from the system set in place in Florence by Francesco de' Medici. On both sides of the Alps, indeed, princely collections were difficult to dissociate from this twofold quest, at once physical and metaphysical, which also provided the motivation – as we shall see later – for private collectors. Though perhaps larger and more ostentatious, the northern collections were fundamentally no different in this respect from their southern counterparts – and the parallels are even more striking when one realizes that most princely collections were far smaller than those described above. Alongside Munich, Ambras and Prague – not forgetting the imposing *Kunstkammer* of the Elector of Saxony in Dresden, founded in 1560 and comprising seven galleries housing principally scientific objects but also paintings and curiosities – were more modest cabinets created between the 1560s and the end of the sixteenth century.

THE GREEN VAULTS

One of the very rare royal collections to have survived largely intact is that of the Electors of Saxony at Dresden. Founded in 1560 by the elector Augustus, it was housed in a series of rooms in the palace called the 'Grüne Gewolbe', or Green Vaults. Augustus (opposite) is shown wearing ceremonial armour and holding his sword of office. The collection contained some *naturalia* but much more *artificialia* – clocks, scientific instruments, automata, turned ivory, items connected with medicine, printing and hunting and works of art and jewelry. ABOVE Setting to hold a cherry stone carved with thirty miniscule heads.

> – *Letter from Galileo describing Tasso's*
> Gerusalemme Liberata
>
> *It is like entering the study of some little man with a taste for curios who has amazed himself by fitting it out with things that have something strange about them, but are, as a matter of fact nothing but bric-a-brac. Here one finds a petrified crab, a dried chameleon, a fly and a spider in gelatine in a fragment of amber, a few of those little clay figurines said to be found in ancient Egyptian tombs.*

Two lidded goblets by Elias
Lenker of Augsburg made before
1629. RIGHT St Christopher
carrying a celestial sphere with
a haloed Christ Child on the top.
OPPOSITE Hercules carrying
a terrestrial globe, inscribed
with the most up-to-date
geographical information.

– Anton Francesco Doni, 1552

I went to see a collection of antiquities, and he who showed it to me is in my opinion madder than I am myself. He began by showing me a marble head, praising it to me as the most stupendous thing in the world, then various busts, feet, hands, and fragments, a sack of medals, a little chest of bizarre things, a stone crab, a piece of wood which is half wood and half the most solid rock [i.e. fossilized]; certain vases known as lacrimarii, *certain terracotta lamps, cinerary urns, and a thousand other novelties. When I had been there for four hours, and when I saw that he was so deeply in love with these bits of stone, I said to him:*
'Oh, if you had been the owner of these things when they were complete, eh?'
'Oh God, what pleasure I would have had',
he replied.
'And if you had seen them as they are now?'
'I would have died', said the noble man.

A carved ivory olifant or hunting horn, probably from Muslim Sicily, *c.* 1100, acquired by the Elector for his *Kunstkammer*. Such horns were prized by collectors because of their association with the story of Roland.

RIGHT Unicorn from a German bestiary published in Strasbourg, 1546.

These also included the collections of the Landgraves of Hesse at Kassel (*c.* 1577, reorganized in the 1590s), the Dukes of Wurttemberg in Stuttgart (*c.* 1600), the Electors of Brandenburg in Berlin (first inventory dating from 1599) and that of the Danish kings in Copenhagen (first mentioned during the reign of Frederick II, 1559–88). In the majority of cases, however, this first generation of *Kunstkammern* suffered the full force of the destruction wrought by the Thirty Years' War, and the cult of curiosities was only to blossom fully from the mid-seventeenth century.

It is of course impossible to reduce the history of the cult of curiosities and its greatest collectors to a single narrative thread. More than any other perhaps, this was a sensibility that was the product of remarkable minds and individual psychologies, of exceptional fortunes and destinies, and of a particular spirit of emulation specific to a single country, region or even city. Yet at the same time it is also impossible to deny that representatives of the last of the three or four generations that marked the flowering and decline of the cult of the collector were increasingly unambiguous in their pursuit of the bizarre for its own sake. In so doing, they also discovered the values of the Baroque after their own fashion, and facilitated the emergence of a new type of collector. Henceforth, the point of the exercise was not so much to gather together the elements for a future investigation, objects forming part of an as yet unfinished whole (as had been the concern, at least in part, of collectors such as Aldrovandi and Imperato), but rather to cultivate all that was intriguing and mysterious.

Three more treasures from the Grüne Gewolbe of Dresden.

OPPOSITE An owl in gold, enamel, agate and diamonds made by Gottfried Döring in Dresden before 1718.

LEFT Goblet in the form of a black girl made of rhinoceros horn holding a shell on which is perched a dragon holding a miniature elephant, made about 1709.

BELOW A winged dragon made of pearl, enamel and various minerals. The creature has its mouth open, displaying teeth and tongue; made before 1706.

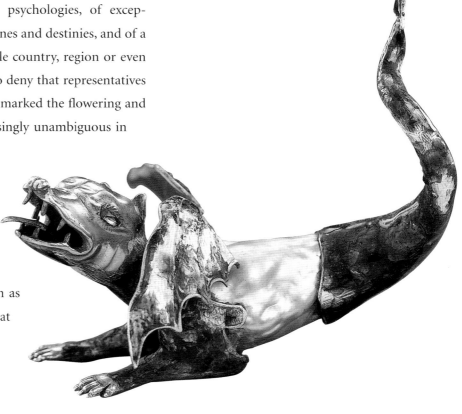

The Collectors 181

Attention has rightly been drawn to the similarity of spirit between the collectors of the late seventeenth century and the writings of the great rhetorician Emanuele Tesauro.[42] If he took as his title for his most celebrated work *The Aristotelian Telescope* (*Il Cannochiale aristotelico*, Turin, 1675), it was in order – significantly – to lament the fact that the telescope diminished the mystery of creation. Like a dislocation or slippage of the visible world, an all-embracing double game or double meaning, every outward appearance opened up a fresh meaning while also concealing it, and revealed rhetorical 'conceits' of nature ('*argutezze della natura*') and so many references to a metaphorical game of infinite and ever-hidden meaning.

Already numerous in the sixteenth century, by the seventeenth century encyclopaedic collections in Europe could thus be counted in their hundreds. Over the decades, scholars and connoisseurs either superseded princes in the role of collector or pursued the activity in parallel. In many cases, on the death of their owners these private collections were bought by local magnates and subsumed into their dynastic collections, and so the twin traditions of the cult of curiosities eventually merged into one. Paradoxically, as Adalgisa Lugli has pointed out, the waning of encyclopaedic collections in Europe during the Enlightenment was virtually contemporaneous with the ambitious project of the *Encyclopédie*.

Doubtless many aspects of the psychology of collecting respond to psychoanalytical exegesis, just as they corresponded to the medieval and Renaissance theory of the humours; doubtless it is easy to discern in this activity symptoms of obsession or depression, or mechanisms of cleavage and defence. But psychogenetic explanations and theories of cause and effect can only ever offer a partial justification, one-sided and linear, of phenomena, leaving the fundamental mystery virtually untouched. What do we really know of the evolution of patterns, of the interdependence of impulses, of unexpected collusions, of the unpredictable drifts and currents which precipitate us into esoteric tastes that must be satisfied, into frenzied quests and the cult of curiosities? At the very most, we may append ourselves as the newest and latest addition to the anatomy of this 'passion', and to the make-up of the collector: a melancholic tropism, permeating and uniting the other necessary characteristics: an enquiring mind; a penchant for secrecy; a propensity for rationalization; a passion for the process of acquisition; a fascination for the transmutation of forms and hybrids; and an inexhaustible ability to question the boundaries between life and death, the nature of being and the evanescence of life. Together these obsessions transform cabinets of curiosities into places of mourning as much as of jubilation, imbued with the sole conviction that 'Man is a Noble Animal, splendid in ashes, and pompous in the Grave' (*Urn Burial*).

The concept of the cabinet of curiosities
began to change when differences became
more important than correspondences.
This would lead to the breaking up of
the great collections and their re-allocation
to specialized institutions, the *naturalia*
to natural history museums and the
artificialia to art galleries.
The collection of Joseph Bonnier de
la Mosson stands between these two worlds.
His house in the rue Saint-Dominique in
Paris was filled with a mass of disparate
objects in the tradition of the *Kunstkammer*.
The difference was that they were strictly
segregated, their didactic purpose taking
precedence over the sense of the marvellous.
In 1739 a pictorial record was made showing
how the collection was displayed (pp. 188–89).
A few years earlier the artist Jacques de Lajoue
had recreated it in a more fanciful style,
transforming it into a Rococo dream (left).
Both, however, make it clear that the
arrangement was highly systematic. Shown
here are the cases devoted to lenses and,
below, regular solids and machines.

BONNIER DE LA MOSSON

Bonnier de la Mosson's brother-in-law was the Duc de Picquigny, also a keen collector. For him, too, Lajoue provided a series of paintings which far more obviously go back to the magical atmosphere of the curiosities. His panel called *The Apothecary's Shop*, set in a strange vaulted space, features all the mystic paraphernalia of the *Kunstkammer* – the alligator suspended from the ceiling, the elephant's head, the giant spider, the oriental magician and alchemist's furnace.

The Phantom Cabinet 187

Conrad Gesner (1516–65), prolific writer, scholar and polymath (author of a monumental compendium of forms of animal life entitled *Icones Animalium*, published in three volumes between 1553 and 1560), claimed in his other key work (*Bibliotheca Universalis*, Zurich, 1545),[43] that he had drawn upon no fewer than one thousand eight hundred authors and their works, reducing 'an entire library to a single volume'.

The most recent commentary on the works of Sir Thomas Browne confirms that for the first edition alone of his treatise inquiring into 'Vulgar and Common Errors' (*Pseudodoxia Epidemica*, 1645) he had recourse to two hundred and ten folios, one hundred and twenty quartos and one hundred and twenty others in smaller format, and that for subsequent editions he made reference to a further seventy-five volumes in addition.

The cult of curiosities was a cult of summation, of the sum total of things, of juxtaposition and addition repeated *ad infinitum*; the Age of Enlightenment, to reiterate a contrast that is now time-honoured, adopted a stance at the opposite extreme, placing itself firmly on the side of universality, of a hierarchical world view, and of an assumption of the validity of the broader categories of reason.[44] After 1750, the collector of curiosities and 'patient pedant', as represented by Sir Thomas Browne, was to give way to the Encyclopaedists, who dismissed the naivety and archaic approach of their predecessors with withering scorn: Aldrovandi, Gesner and Kircher were now relegated to the past, and their places were taken by Linnaeus (the first edition of whose *System of Nature* had appeared in 1735), Cuvier and Buffon.

The crowded and claustrophobic spaces devoted to 'theatres of the world' dwindled in number, and became fragmented into a series of private cabinets, each devoted to a particular speciality. Justly proud of his achievement, Joseph Bonnier de la Mosson (1702–44), captain of the hunt at the Tuileries and son of the treasurer of the Languedoc, left behind him an impressive record of his collections. These were housed in an enfilade of rooms in his *hôtel particulier* on rue Saint Dominique, devoted successively to anatomy, chemistry, pharmacy, drugs, lathes and specialized tools, natural history ('first cabinet of natural history, containing animals in phials of preserving fluid', 'second cabinet of natural history, containing desiccated animals'), prints and rare books, mechanics and physics. Drawings made of the collections by the architect Jean Baptiste Courtonne in

These drawings by the architect Jean-Baptiste Courtonne (1739) offer a more factual record of Bonnier de la Mosson's collection than Lajoue's flights of fancy. In their entirety they show eight cabinets devoted to anatomy, chemistry, pharmacy, drugs, animals in preserving jars, dried animals, mechanics and books. This section (opposite) displays coral.

The Phantom Cabinet 189

A third record of Bonnier de la Mosson's collection is the catalogue complied by the art-dealer Gersaint (whose main claim to fame is the shop-sign painted for him by Watteau). Gersaint was a pioneer in the publication of illustrated catalogues – Rembrandt's etchings among others – describing himself in one of them as a 'curieux'. His catalogue of Bonnier de la Mosson's collection was compiled in 1744 when it was dispersed on Bonnier's death. It contained detailed reproductions of both natural and artificial objects. This plate shows 'shells, insects and reptiles'.

1739, representing a 'cross section' of the entire contents, when placed end to end, form a sequence almost ten metres in length.

When this collection was dispersed in 1744–5, a catalogue was compiled by Gersaint, who confirmed that 'these cabinets [were] embellished with the most ingenious and delightful items imaginable', adding the following observations on the person responsible for it: 'M. de la Mosson has always taken pleasure in procuring the sight and study of all things he possessed to inquiring spirits, both from among our own people and from abroad, and to come and amuse oneself with him in his cabinet was sufficient to induce in him the obligation to do so. He desired to know every-thing about his purchases, making of this an unwavering principle which yielded great benefits in gaining the understanding that he sought of all things....'

The very proportions of these spaces, the design of their panel-ling and cabinets, the height of the rooms, the unabashed wealth of their ornamentation and the refinement of their architectural design and motifs were sufficient in themselves, as we have seen, to mark the contrast between them and the *musaeum clausum* of collectors such as Settala and Aldrovandi. The arcane motives and naive beliefs of the previous century shrank back in the face of the new scientific instruments and a belief in the validity of aesthetic pleasure for its own sake. 'Here is one of the finest cabinets in Paris,' declared de la Mosson's contemporary Dezallier d'Argenville, 'both in its arrangement and in the beautiful things it contains.... Seven rooms of lofty height and arranged *en enfilade* form a charming sight.'[45] About this sump-tuous and sophisticated décor, there hung, in short, only the faintest whiff of the cult of curiosities (emblematic images of which continued neverthe-less to fascinate Bonnier de la Mosson, from the shells that served as fron-tispieces to his catalogues to ivory pyramids or paper-thin goblets turned in wood). Viewed with detached amusement, a degree of nostalgia and dis-creet astonishment, the cult of curiosities now faded into the background.

It was a background that found echoes within the cabinet itself: the series of overdoors painted by Jacques de Lajoue (?1686–1761) for four of the rooms plucked some of the collection's exhibits out of their context in order to insert them into a set of architectural flights of fancy; in so doing, they definitively transported the collections into the realm of the imagination, plunging them into a diaphanous light and a dream-like atmosphere.

Similarly, the thirteen paintings executed by Lajoue for Bonnier de la Mosson's brother-in-law the Duc de Picquigny (1714–69), a decade or so his junior and his disciple in matters of taste, unambiguously single out the most fetishistic items in his collection (notably the salamander, the armadillo, the coral and the suspended alligator) in order to place them in a fantastical décor, an extravaganza of rococo swirls and volutes, their swooping lines echoed by the curves and counter-curves of the frame (as in *The Apothecary's Shop*). Painted between 1734 and 1737, these panels were immediately engraved, and through this medium became a remarkable success.[46] Three of them – *The Sea*, *Astronomy* and *Forces of Movement* – repeat titles and themes used by Lajoue in his paintings for Bonnier de la Mosson.

Foreshortened perspectives, formal allusions and quotations, pictures within pictures: clearly the cult of curiosities was now nothing more than an image concealed within others, the focus of imaginative extravaganzas. (Or indeed of speculation: 'our nobles', observed Louis-Sébastien Mercier (1740–1814) in his *Tableau de Paris* (1781), 'under the guise of being collectors of curiosities, are in fact dealers in second-hand goods on a magnificent scale, who, without need and without passion, and solely in order to make money, buy jewels, horses, paintings, prints and antiques; they establish stud farms and cabinets which will soon be shops'.) And by the second half of the eighteenth century, when a connoisseur invited his friends to admire his collections, this performance extended to the ritual of the visit itself. In the engraving that forms the frontispiece to the collection of the connoisseur Rémy (1757–74),beneath the armadillos, diodons (an exotic tropical fish) and crocodiles ritually suspended from the ceiling and amid its preserving jars and stuffed animals, an 'Indian' is thus depicted proudly presenting a shell to the fashionable ladies and inquisitive gentlemen who form the group of visitors. It was now considered the height of good taste for the host to deck himself out in some of the choicest items of ethnographical interest in his collection – feather headdresses, tunics and

Gersaint's trade-card for his own business (1740) is very much in the spirit of cabinets of curiosities.

The Phantom Cabinet 191

the like – in order to provide a running commentary on the history and provenance of each of his objects.

We should not be tempted to over-simplify the multiplicity of reasons that lay behind the progressive *dissociation* of the motives that bound together the culture of curiosities, and the marginalization that then ensued. Doubtless the rise of the spirit of scientific inquiry and the belief in a new rational order were responsible for relegating 'wonders' to the lower slopes of human knowledge; doubtless the pre-eminent status accorded to observation, to new methodologies, and to the accumulation of data reduced the cult of curiosities to the status of an imperfect science. But among all these factors and others, this shift was also the culmination of a transformation of what might be termed the popular imagination, a process that had started in the previous century. The civil wars and violent upheavals that tore Europe apart in the sixteenth and seventeenth centuries brought about a polarization of the values associated with the cult of curiosities, so contributing to its fall in status. The taste for virtuoso but 'sterile' *tours de force*, the reckless expenditure, the fascination with what was secret, the magic or esoteric practices associated with cabinets of curiosities: all these were now viewed as positively undesirable or socially unacceptable, and were dismissed as mere entertainment or naive illusion: 'in positive terms, the regularity of the new natural order mirrored the decorum of the new social order; in negative terms, wonder in natural philosophy smacked of the disruptive forces of enthusiasm and superstition in religion and politics'.[47]

This irrepressible, irreducible capacity to amaze, and the object of curiosity's power of substantial subjugation were now viewed as symptoms of ignorance and superstition, and retained their fascination only for certain social categories, the 'most vulnerable' in society: 'women, the very young, the very old, primitive people, and the uneducated masses, a motley group collectively designated as "the vulgar".'[48] It was thus a whole new philosophy of the nature of truth, developed in the first half of the eighteenth century, that marginalized and dispelled the charm of the cult of curiosities. There was no place for the inexplicable or the bizarre in a culture that demanded, then as now, a reality that was on the way to being

MR GREENE'S MUSEUM

An ambitious private museum of the 18th century was that of Mr Greene in Lichfield (above). Dr Johnson visited it in March 1776. 'It was', writes Boswell, 'a truly wonderful collection, both of antiquities and natural curiosities, and ingenious works of art. He had all the articles accurately arranged, with their names upon labels, printed at his own little press.'

By the mid-18th century, collecting had lost most of its esoteric associations and had become part of the status-symbolism of the wealthy. In this engraving (opposite), the connoisseur Rémy may be the 'Indian' showing a shell to some ladies.

explained, a reality with no parts left over or superfluities; henceforth, a predictable nature would obey the laws of probability, leaving no room for exceptions, just as the 'mediocrity' demanded by society left no room for gratuitous excess ('the metaphysical shift from marvellous to uniform nature paralleled a shift in cultural values from princely magnificence to bourgeois domesticity').[49]

Hence the staggering rarity of curiosities became ever more relative, and their singularity steadily less remarkable; surprise and a fascination for wonders were reduced to a craving for the sensational, a taste which was henceforth to find expression in the phenomena of travelling fairs and the popular press. It was a distant America, certainly, but none the less a real one that was conjured up by the 'Indian' in the drawing room; and a visit to a collection was now not so much a revelation, or a unique experience, but rather an educational form of entertainment, a form of that well-bred didacticism that inspired writers throughout Europe at this period, from the Frenchman Fontenelle to the cosmopolitan Italian Francesco Algarotti, author of the famous *Newtonism for Ladies*.

Within the context of this new structure of reality, objects which had hitherto been jumbled together or juxtaposed in the cabinet of curiosities now had to be distinguished; that is to say it became necessary to sort and arrange according to a new scale of values. The first step was to abandon the confusion of *naturalia* and *artificialia*, and to separate works of art from works of science; the next was to draw a distinction within the category of works of art between major and minor works, and between fine and decorative art, the latter being a superior form of craftsmanship distinguished by the excellence and virtuoso skill of its execution. As in certain pathologies of a linguistic nature, the first thing to vanish was the very *syntax* of the cabinet. An exemplary illustration of this dispersal or dislocation is to be found in the transfer of the Habsburg collections: the paintings and alabaster urns are now on display in the Kunsthistorisches Museum in Vienna, a treasure house of great art, while the gilded rhinoceros horns have been consigned to the provincial castle of Ambras, so bringing the picturesque and the bizarre together.[50] With the disintegration of the 'impure' space of the cabinet of curiosities in the second half of the seventeenth century, there emerged the topography of art with which

STRAWBERRY HILL

With Horace Walpole's Strawberry Hill at Twickenham, near London, we move from the pseudo-science of the *Kunstkammer* to the pseudo-history of the Gothic Revival. Walpole's ambition was to re-create the Middle Ages in miniature. His collection – suits of armour, illuminated manuscripts, furniture, stained glass – was dictated by literary imagination rather than by the urge to understand the cosmos. His *Castle of Otranto* was the first Gothic novel and Strawberry Hill (opposite) the pioneer of Neo-Gothic architecture.

Denon retained a feeling for the magical aura surrounding the remains of remarkable people. This pseudo-medieval reliquary was made to hold the relics of El Cid and Ximenes, Abelard and Héloise, Ines de Castro and Henri IV.

we are now familiar, as well as a new nomenclature and bounds of taste which were to remain unquestioned for the two following centuries (a fact that was self-evidently one of the reasons behind the resurgence of the older concept, as we shall see, in contemporary art).

The version (or aspect) of the culture of curiosities deemed admissible by the Age of Enlightenment had undergone a definitive shift in emphasis. No longer was it concerned with a taste for rarity, nor with the *minutiae* that Kant contrasted with the Sublime, the true source of aesthetic emotion: a singular or sophisticated taste, the expression of a unique personality, as defined by its transcendence over the average sensibility, and the interest it accorded the undervalued forms – disregarded or disparaged – on the fringes of art. According to this view, the great English collectors of the eighteenth century, Walpole and Beckford – conspicuous eccentrics and precursors of dandyism and aestheticism – may be seen as continuing or adapting the culture of curiosities. Each appointed a place specifically for the purpose – respectively Strawberry Hill and Fonthill Abbey – and withdrew within its walls; each of these eccentric residences found its justification wholly in the collections it housed; and these collections consisted largely of items that defied the aesthetic norms then current, implying a higher degree of aesthetic sensibility. These sanctuaries were also endowed with something of the aura of mystery that surrounded cabinets of curiosities, but the only cult now celebrated within their walls was that of art as such, and of memory.

Another example of this transference of values is to be found in the person of Vivant Denon (1747–1825).[51] A leading figure in fashionable circles, sometime diplomat, accomplished courtier, draughtsman and engraver, he was by turns an agent of the monarchy, spy for the Republic and administrator of the Empire. Known for many years only as the (disputed) author of a short story entitled *Point de lendemain* (*No Tomorrow*), in recent times he has assumed a new and more distinguished stature: his role in the cultural politics of the Empire, and hence in the foundation of the Louvre, the part he played in the Egyptian campaign, and the altogether exceptional and picaresque nature of his life have all found a particular resonance in the contemporary imagination. Beneath his chameleon-like exterior, Denon was essentially an amateur in the fullest sense of the term, as well as a passionate collector. Having retired from public life on 3 October

1815, he devoted his last ten years to perfecting the contents and décor of his collections, housed in his apartments on quai Voltaire, a visit to which rapidly became *de rigueur* for the cultivated classes, inspiring accounts by literary figures including Bernardin de Saint-Pierre, Madame de Senlis and Lady Morgan.

Quantities of paintings, sculptures and engravings were to be found within this treasure store: the three volumes of the catalogue compiled for the sale of the collection list no fewer than 1,574 works by Callot, 133 by Marc Antonio Raimondi, and dozens by Rembrandt and Parmigianino. But it was Denon's fascination with Antiquity and with Egypt, fostered by his travels, that accentuated the parallels between the contents of his cabinet and that of a *Wunderkammer*, as described in a recent commentary: 'There one beheld mummies of animals, a human head that had once belonged to a mummy, a beautifully worked female mask, Egyptian paintings, a papyrus bearing a text in hieroglyphs, and a superb painting of the judgement of Osiris in four tones, azure blue, terracotta, green and yellow. Other display cabinets contained figurines in bronze and glazed

GOODRICH COURT

Like many Romantic collectors, Sir Samuel Rush Meyrick combined the genuine and the make-believe. His castle of Goodrich Court, built in a remote part of Britain near Wales, was a full-blooded exercise in the Gothic Revival. But his collection consisted of real medieval objects, like this 16th-century Limoges enamel inkstand featuring the life of Hercules.

SOANE AND DENON

Sir John Soane, the leading British Neo-classical architect, turned his own house in London into a museum. Its interiors are a wholly personal creation of small, shadowy rooms opening off one another and leading into strangely conceived, architecturally allusive spaces at different levels, filled (and over-filled) with items from his collection. Soane was not interested in shells and minerals. He bought mostly fragments of classical buildings and sculpture and paintings; the single most important object was an ancient Egyptian sarcophagus. It is the way everything is crowded together that gives it its *Kunstkammer* atmosphere. Soane, however, was not a magus or a mystic but a Romantic of the 19th century.

The collection of Vivant Denon (opposite), the nucleus of the Napoleonic Louvre, bears a superficial resemblance to Soane's house, but Denon's was the approach of a modern museum curator rather than that of a Romantic artist. The setting is not realistic, but is due to the imagination of the painter Benjamin Zix. Despite appearances, his mission was to classify and to document.

CAMPAGNE
EN EGYPTE

CAMPAGNE
EN ITALIE EN
ALLEMAGNE

terracotta, amulets, sparrowhawks representing gods and goddesses, vultures, and a wooden hand holding a scroll.'[52]

At the heart of this remarkable Aladdin's cave, with its items representing every moment of consequence in an exceptional life, lay an object that was even more singular, seeming to represent the quintessence of the collection as a whole: 'a reliquary, hexagonal in form and Gothic in style, flanked at its angles by six small turrets linked by flying buttresses to a crowning piece composed of a small edifice surmounted by a cross: the two principal faces of this reliquary were each divided into six compartments, containing the following objects: fragments of bones belonging to El Cid and Ximenes, found in their tombs at Burgos; fragments of the bones of Héloise and Abelard, taken from their tombs at the Paraclete; hairs belonging to Agnès Sorel, buried at Loches, and to Inès de Castro, buried at Alcobaça; part of the moustache of Henri IV, King of France, discovered intact on the exhumation of the bodies of the kings at Saint-Denis in 1793; fragment of the shroud of Turenne; fragment of the bones of Molière and La Fontaine; hairs belonging to General Desaix.

Two of the lateral faces of the same item are filled: one with the autograph signature of Napoleon; the other with a bloodstained fragment of the chemise he was wearing when he died, a lock of his hair, and a leaf from the willow tree beneath which he is buried on the island of St Helena.'[53]

In this bizarre object, believed to have been lost for ever until it was discovered recently,[54] we see a veritable work *in reductio*, evincing a taste for miniaturization and saturation, but also and more importantly a passion for relics, essentially secular in nature, and bringing together the scattered fragments of memorable corpses. The place once occupied by occult knowledge and the mastery of the hidden forces of nature, of crossbreeds and hybrids, is here taken by a fascination with history, as embodied in its heroes, as well as with the fragility and vulnerability of the human body. All that persists from one culture to the next, and from one paradigm to its successor, is a diffuse belief in a mnemonic power, in the obscure capacity of images and bodies to retain and manifest the aura of a presence (a notion curiously similar to the 'mnemonic energies' of which Aby Warburg postulated the existence in certain images deeply rooted in western culture).[55]

Meyrick's main interest was in metalwork, particularly armour; he was put in charge of the armouries of the Tower of London and Windsor Castle. His own collection has been dispersed, but his catalogue remains as a record. ABOVE Copy of a Greek or Roman oil lamp. OPPOSITE Helmet and chain-mail.

If something of the 'spirit' of curiosity lingered on in Denon's bizarre conglomeration, it was to make its reappearance in definitively 'fossilized' form in the shape of documents or quotations in the other site of major significance in this nineteenth-century chronicle: the 'medieval' manor house of Goodrich Court, a combination of Gothic and Sir Walter Scott, built in Herefordshire by Sir Samuel Rush Meyrick (1783–1848).

Trained as a lawyer, Meyrick inherited a considerable fortune following the deaths of his father and brother, which enabled him to indulge his passion – singular but in tune with the spirit of the time – for medieval myth and legend, and in particular the heraldry and armour of the Middle Ages. In 1810 he was made a fellow of the Society of Antiquaries in London, and ten years later he had accumulated such quantities of armour that it took over the attic, the staircases and even the bedchambers of his London residence, and attracted distinguished visitors including Delacroix and Bonnington. The publication in 1823 of his three-volume *Critical Inquiry into Ancient Armour as it existed in Europe but Particularly in England* not only sealed Meyrick's reputation, but also earned him the respect and friendship of Sir Walter Scott, as well as a commission to reorganize the armouries in the Tower of London and Windsor Castle.

Following the example of Scott, 'lord of the manor' of Abbotsford, in 1828 Meyrick conjured up – with the assistance of the architect Edward Blore – a veritable medieval castle, another 'romance in lime and stone', for the exclusive purpose of housing his collections (indeed he designed the disposition of each object, down to the smallest dagger or gauntlet, and it was upon the plates devoted to the castle that the construction of the actual rooms was later based).

It was the collection of armour at Goodrich Court that earned this mock-medieval fantasy a place in the history of curiosities. As he pursued

SIR ASHTON LEVER

The Leverian Museum, creation of Sir Ashton Lever, was installed in a suite of rooms in his house in Leicester Square, London, in 1775. It consisted chiefly of *naturalia* and he called it his 'Holophusicon' Museum (meaning 'All Nature'). Open to the public every day on a commercial basis, it contained thousands of objects – fossils, shells, birds, insects, reptiles, fishes, monkeys and (the prize exhibits) an elephant and a zebra – and became a popular attraction. A character in Maria Edgeworth's *Belinda* throws aside a letter from a friend because 'I saw something about the Leverian Museum, and a swallow's nest in a pair of garden shears; and I was afraid I was to have a catalogue of curiosities, for which I have little taste and less time'. When Sir Ashton died in 1788 it was sold (by a lottery) and moved to another location (see p. 206).

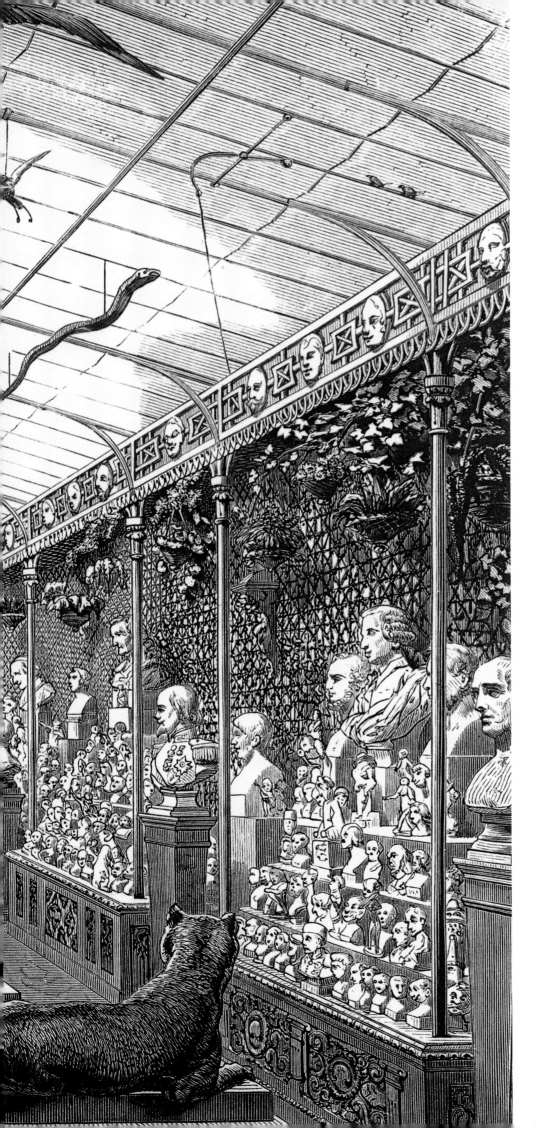

The sculptor Jean-Pierre Dantan (1800–69) was a friend of Victor Hugo, Liszt and Chopin, of whom he left remarkable caricature portraits. Keenly interested in phrenology, he made grotesque and 'ironic' busts, earning him the title of 'the drawing-room Phidias'. He published two books, *Dantanorama* (1833) and *Museum Dantan* (1838). His studio was located in the district known as New Athens, in northern Paris, where there were unexpected reminders of the cabinet of curiosities, such as the crocodile hanging from the ceiling.

The Leverian Museum's second home was the Rotunda, south of the Thames in Blackfriars Bridge Road. Here further ethnographical material was added to it, including objects brought back from the South Seas by Captain Cook. It finally closed in 1806.

In America the collection of natural history was taken up with enthusiasm, often with patriotic overtones. The artist Charles Willson Peale created a museum of American flora and fauna (opposite), and painted himself drawing a curtain to reveal it (1822). In the background are cases of stuffed birds, in the foreground an American turkey and mastodon bones that Peale himself had helped to excavate (the subject of an earlier painting by him).

his researches into the subject, Meyrick came to realize that the idea of amassing and exhibiting armour as so many examples of virtuoso craftsmanship or impressive showpieces could be traced back to Charles V, who had chosen to assemble his collection at Ambras, where his work was continued and expanded by his brother and successor Ferdinand I and later by Archduke Ferdinand II (1529–95). 'While Ferdinand was governor of Bohemia,' Meyrick went on, 'between 1547 and 1563, he began collecting on a large scale in Bohemia, his special interest being armour. On the one hand, coats of arms represented for him the historical personality of their one-time owners, and on the other, he valued them as objects that reminded him of the events at which they had been worn. They constituted an imaginary collection of heroes, which he later called his "honourable company". While he was in the Tirol, the Archduke was

KEY HOLE OF THE ENTRANCE HALL AT GOODRICH COURT

Even the keyhole of Goodrich Court was mock-medieval though by no means a slavish imitation.

gradually able to arrange his collections [...] in Ambras castle [...]. In the kunstkammer a series of ancient objects was included which had belonged to his great forebears.'[56]

The arrangement of the armour collection at Ambras thus provided the direct inspiration for Goodrich Court: a purely literary inspiration, as Meyrick was never able to visit Ambras, and had to content himself with reconstructing it in his imagination from the engravings and treatises in his library. From armour there was a 'natural' progression to 'curiosities and antiquities'. While the entrance hall at Goodrich Court was, needless to say, in the medieval style or spirit, the lamp that lit the great staircase was 'of Greek art and made for the Romans, as it was dug out of the ruins of Herculaneum [...]. The female masks and horses' heads with which it is adorned are in the very best style, as well as the Janus head, which forms the lid.' The hall opened into an antechamber, followed by an 'Asiatic' armoury, embellished with tiles from the Alhambra and wallpaper of Persian inspiration. Also on the ground floor were an extraordinary hall containing a reconstruction of a tournament, a chapel, a library, a large drawing room and a breakfast room, the latter in the Queen Anne style (very advanced for the period) and decorated with Dresden and Sèvres porcelain.

On the first floor, a James I hall was followed by one devoted to Charles I, the 'Prince's Bedchamber', another bedchamber furnished in 'modern French style', and another in Greek style containing numerous Greek and Etruscan urns and vases. Thus Meyrick's omnivorous and insatiable curiosity created in Goodrich Court one of the earliest and most spectacular expressions of what was later to flourish as *fin-de-siècle* eclecticism.

But to return for a moment to the ground floor, it was in the accumulation of items in the South Seas Room that the heritage of the cabinet of curiosities was most directly to be felt, for this was 'filled with rude weapons, feathered cloaks, etc. of the islanders of the Pacific Ocean. Among them is a war cloak made from the plumage of the Tropic bird, brought from the Sandwich Isles by Captain Cook...'. It is perplexing, at the very least, for the modern mind to attempt to detect the thread or logic to link together these disparate objects: doubtless these *ethnographica* which would have entranced Kircher or Elias Ashmole were included here by analogy with

Ambras, as well as in the desire to reconstruct a comprehensive history of arms and armour. In truth, the theme of the cabinet of curiosities reappears here only incidentally, through the device of a welter of singular objects which belonged first and foremost to the field of warfare.

This succession of disparate spaces, inspired by a (new) desire to reconstruct the past, is in fact, as has been noted elsewhere, the precursor of the 'period rooms' of modern museums. In a way, the wheel has turned full circle: the metaphorical games, the dizzying heights of analogy which flourished in every possible form in the cabinet of curiosities now find their contrast and opposite in these mnemonic blocks, fragments of a décor or moment, driven henceforth by a passion for 'historical veracity'. The dream of knowledge in all its forms has now yielded once and for all to that of history: as Clive Wainwright concludes, Sir Walter Scott at Abbotsford and Samuel Rush Meyrick at Goodrich Court sought above all 'to reintroduce into their seats the pomp and splendour that they imagined had once existed'.

Resurgences:
the Spirit of Curiosity

Poised between life and death, the ape that
adorns the cabinet of the English collector
and antiquary Alistair McAlpine is a potent
symbol. '*Ars scimmia natura*' – art is the ape
of nature, said the ancients, a suggestion that
lovers of curiosities could have easily inverted,
fascinated as they were by nature imitating art.
Almost as startling as the ape in this picture,
the last few decades have seen a resurgence
that emulates (or recreates) that theatre of
imitation between art and nature that
cabinets represented. Visible across several
art movements of the the 20th century, from
Surrealism to contemporary art, the aesthetic
of the cabinet of curiosities has also inspired
a great many everyday interiors, throughout
Europe, since the 1970s. To the Surrealists'
beloved theme of the incongruous object, and
to the concerns of space, context and framing
that play a key role in contemporary art, can
be added these scenes of domestic decoration,
singular works in themselves, albeit invisible
because of their private nature. That a
number of these 'inventors' are also lovers
of engravings, perhaps familiar from
catalogues of the 16th and 17th centuries,
is only one of the reasons or motivations
behind this remarkable resurgence.

An old collector

Venerated but relegated to an occasional footnote, in the modern world the cabinet of curiosities now survives only marginally in histories of science or magic, disregarded by all but a handful of collectors with a particular interest in eccentric objects and crucial turning points in the history of art (a full re-evaluation of Mannerism and the Baroque was only achieved in the early decades of the twentieth century, as we know, thanks to the analyses of Wolffin and his fellow historians in Vienna). Thus the spirit of curiosity appears once again at the turn of the nineteenth and twentieth centuries, in the work of Henry-René D'Allemagne 1863–1950), a little-known but prolific scholar and an insatiable collector.

A librarian at the Arsenal who almost certainly also enjoyed a substantial private fortune, D'Allemagne has left behind a strange body of work, collected and bound in a series of sumptuous quarto editions. A few hundred copies of each were printed, under his direction and for the most part privately (a fact which has earned him a place in French bibliographical history, as these lavishly illustrated volumes offer a valuable, and frequently unique, documentary record of the subjects they address). He was obviously fascinated by objects from the past which most clearly retained the imprint and the perfume of their history: objects used in daily life, as necessary as they are insignificant. He devoted volumes which still stand as works of reference to such things as playing cards,[57] toys and lamps.[58]

The three volumes that he devoted to objects of daily life[59] indisputably offer the most striking demonstration of D'Allemagne's obsession with the past: a teeming diorama of life in earlier times, the work presents an extraordinary assemblage of kitchen utensils, fans, gaming sets and sewing boxes, musical boxes and tools answering all needs and uses. Ironwork was accorded a place of special importance, in this work as in D'Allemagne's collection (he was to devote no fewer than three books to the subject, in 1891, 1902 and 1943, not to mention numerous chapters in his other books). The virtuoso craftsmanship of these objects, on the borderline between 'art' and technique, naturally encouraged comparisons with the technical *tours de force* assembled in cabinets of curiosities, and was an early indication of D'Allemagne's interest in the subject.

It would appear that a large part, if not the majority, of the hundreds of items of which photographs are reproduced in his books came from his

HENRY D'ALLEMAGNE

Part of the wall at the end of the 'grand bureau' (above), on the first floor of Henry D'Allemagne's house. It gives only a faint impression of the extraordinary accumulation and combination of elements which occupied every square inch of the corridor. Inspired by early 16th-century examples, the walls were covered with canvasses painted in *trompe l'oeil*. Credence tables from the time of Henri IV and marriage chests mingled with late 16th-century chairs. Sculptures in wood, stone and bronze stood next to brass-work and antique locks.

The show-case (left) occupied the space between two windows: it held caskets, table clocks, secular and religious bronzes of the 15th and 16th centuries.

BRETON AND THE SURREALISTS

André Breton in his flat, rue
Blanche, in Paris, photographed
by Gesela Freund. Breton had been
a collector all his life, painstakingly
juxtaposing objects of all sorts
from all over the world – African,
Oceanic, Surrealist, vernacular,
magical – on the walls of his
study. Recognized as something
altogether extraordinary, this
assemblage has been preserved
and is displayed in the
Pompidou Centre, Paris.

own collection, and that in his view (as in Meyrick's) virtually anything was collectable. Like Meyrick, he lived in a fascinating house-cum-museum which embraced every style from Gothic to Louis XV, and from French provincial craftsmanship to Syrian marquetry, crowning his published works with two volumes, one of text and the other of plates, devoted to his extraordinary store of treasures. *La maison d'un vieux collectionneur,* published in 1948, forms part of a tradition (life through objects as much as the life of the objects) stretching from the brothers Goncourt to Mario Praz (though lacking their style), and places the D'Allemagne collection in history, associating it with the *Wunderkammern* whose existence it recalls. Some of the plates depicting D'Allemagne's collection – more reminiscent as they are to contemporary eyes of the unrestrained mania for bric-à-brac that gripped the early years of the twentieth century – seem to offer an involuntary evocation (similar to Proust's contemporary concept of involuntary memory) of a cabinet of curiosities. But in this instance it is merely one possibility among others, a hypothetical possibility of which we seek above all to amass as many examples as possible; here the cabinet of curiosities is no more than one reconstructed scenario among many others, just as it may prompt an anecdote or aside in the text of a scholar, another manifestation of the amateur.

The object made mysterious

Let us now turn to a lengthy description provided by André Breton for the readers of *La semaine de Paris* in 1936: 'The Charles Ratton gallery, 14 rue de Marignan, invites us today, 22 May 1936, to a private view of its exhibition of Surrealist objects. Among some two hundred entries in the catalogue, we find "natural objects", minerals (crystals containing water one hundred thousand years old), plants (carnivorous species), animals (giant anteater, an egg laid by one "oexpyorhix"), "interpretations of natural objects" (a monkey among ferns) or "incorporated" into sculptures, and "disrupted objects" (that is, modified by natural forces, fires, storms, etc.). Here, revealed for the first time to the public, are several objects from Picasso's studio, which take their place, historically, alongside the celebrated "ready-mades" and "assisted ready-mades" of Marcel Duchamp, also on display. Finally, so-called "savage" objects, the finest fetishes and masks from the Americas and Oceania, selected from Charles Ratton's private collection.

The "mathematical objects" are astonishing incarnations in concrete form of the subtlest problems of three-dimensional geometry, while the "found objects" and "interpreted found objects" lead us to the "surrealist objects" proper.'[60] The line of descent or affinity between the possible contents of a cabinet of curiosities and this litany of the odd, unusual and weird – all of it belonging unambiguously to the physical and mental space of modernism, somewhere between Duchamp's 'ready-mades' and Picasso's exotic objects – now emerges with luminous clarity. A number of Surrealists, starting with Breton and Eluard, were avid collectors, a fact which is not surprising given that from the outset the object *qua* object, whether mundane or exotic, craft or art, in its natural state or combined with others, played a role of fundamental importance in the sensibility and aesthetic of Surrealism.

For this position of central significance there was naturally a price to be paid in terms of a precise definition: just as important as the reality of the object was its 'internal representation', the shadow it cast over the psychic world, the 'image presented to the spirit' or nature 'in its relationship with the inner consciousness'.[61] The essential effect of this duality was 'an extremely unfamiliar sensation, of an exceptionally disquieting and complex nature', or 'a disorientation of feeling'.

This 'property of strangeness' possessed by the object has always lain at the heart of the culture of curiosities: the 'accidental' or secondary character of all that is rare, and hence rarely seen; a discreet charm but an essential one amid the motives driving the collector, who sought to amaze others quite as much as he yearned to be amazed himself. Paradoxically, the strangeness of any object in a cabinet of curiosities was the surest guarantee of a sort of reality: the reality of distant cultures, of which it offered living proof, or of the shadowy realm of hidden pockets of reality within the natural world itself. Placed centre stage and exaggerated yet further by Surrealism, this ability of the object to go in and out of reality assumed, by contrast, a polemical dimension, a dialectic for questioning the status of reality and all the evidence in its favour. Things, wrote Albert Beguin in a passage singled out by Breton,[62] 'summarily grouped according to laws that defy formulation – those of external accidents or imponderable and arbitrary leaps of the unconscious – are torn from their mundane, everyday significance and *mysti-fied*, made free once more and capable of assuming a meaning that is mysterious and irrational: what is made mysterious [...] is "reality", the many-sided phenomenon that a transcendental irony destroys by fire'.

In its tireless efforts to 'discredit the things and creatures of reason', Surrealism rediscovered, one after another, all the variables of the culture of curiosities, in order to liberate their potential value. First among these was the essentially non-functional nature of the object. As early as 1924, Breton proposed to make 'some of those objects to which we come close only in dreams and which appear as indefensible on the grounds of utility as on those of decorativeness' (*Introduction au discours sur le peu de réalité*); a decade later, he dreamed of 'machines of highly skilled construction and no useful purpose', of 'plans of immense cities which [...] we will always feel ourselves incapable of founding' and of 'absurd and highly sophisticated automata which would be incapable of doing anything as well as a human being':[63] impossible contraptions which would naturally

The Surrealist exhibition at the Charles Ratton Gallery, Paris, in 1936, photographed by Man Ray.

occupy a place of honour among the many useless objects essential to good order of any cabinet of curiosities.

With its culture of extravagance, its rejection of ordinary common sense and its pointless waste of energy, the Surrealist object was positively furious in its cultivation of the 'disorder' that had been one of the chief reasons for the banishment of cabinets of curiosities from the culture of the Enlightenment. Similarly, another of the principal axes of cabinets of curiosities, namely the capacity and power of metaphorical significance possessed by objects, reappeared in Surrealism under the guise of 'systematic disorder'. While the cabinet of curiosities viewed itself as a theatre of the world, a metaphor of the Creation and hence of the secret harmony of the universe, the Surrealist object 'linked' only two equal phenomena that were dissonant, dissimilar and 'irreconcilable', as Leibniz would have said (the fundamental process of Surrealism, recalled Breton, lending new prominence to Lautréamont, lay in 'the chance encounter of two distant unrealities on unsuitable ground').[64]

Fascinated by the play of correspondences and by the mythology of the occult, Surrealism adopted some of its elements and turned them upside down, inverting its use of metaphor just as Marx had done with dialectic. Far from containing and mirroring the hierarchy of existence, the object was now to play a central role in a 'culture of the effects of systematic disorientation'; pointing towards a different reality, it no longer referred back to the reassuring, sensible world of the divine order, but looked instead to the aberrant, disjointed world of dreams and wonders.

Items of delicacy

While Surrealism rediscovered, indirectly, certain motifs from the cult of curiosities, in the 1940s it fell to a relatively obscure figure to assume the mantle of historian, collector and architect of *Wunderkammern*. Jean-Charles Moreux (1889–1956) began his career in about 1925 as a modernist, but quickly grew weary of a movement that appeared already to consist of the repetitive slogans of dried-out functionalism. In 1937, a 'whirlwind tour of the Veneto' helped to coax him into 'an awareness of his new message'. His appreciation of the works of Palladio; his interest in the history of architecture (the subject of one of his books); his desire to rediscover the use of ornament, and to 'humanize' architecture by playing with scale, optical

ABOVE 'Pan-hoplie', 1953, by André Breton. The line of hieroglyphics at the bottom mean: 'I am shining with love for you.' So Breton explained to his wife, Elise, to whom the collage is dedicated.

OPPOSITE another '*poème–objet*' by André Breton: 'a torn stocking', 1941. This collage, made while Breton was in exile in New York, during the war, is clearly close in spirit to those of Cornell. It belonged to the painter Motta and then to Pierre Matisse.

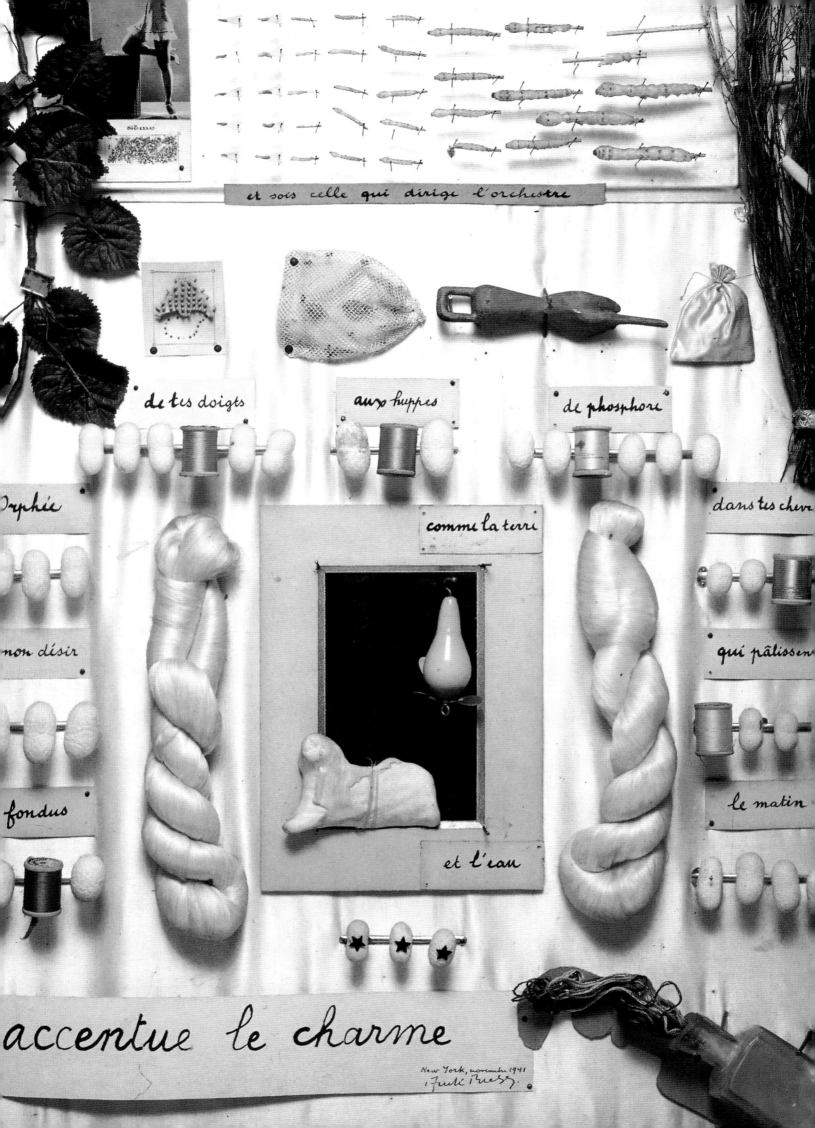

et sois celle qui dirige l'orchestre

de tes doigts   aux huppes   de phosphore

Orphée   comme la terre   dans tes cheve

non désir   qui pâlissen

fondus   le matin

et l'eau

accentue le charme

New York, novembre 1941
André Breton

Jean-Charles Moreux worked in
close collaboration with Bolette
Natanson until her premature
death in 1936; and was rumoured
to be her lover. She belonged to a
famous family of art-lovers and
collectors and herself designed
furniture and other objects. She
shared Moreux's taste for *naturalia*
and incorporated fossils and shells
in their furniture. They travelled
together to add to their collection.
A room in her apartment in the
rue de Chalgrin, Paris (opposite),
uses coral and jellyfish. She opened
her own shop in 1930 where she
showed a table like that in the
foreground. Moreux also set aside
rooms to hold his collection in
his own Paris flat as well as in
his house in the country. The
composition of coral under a glass
globe is by himself and Natanson.

compensation and a reinvented 'picturesque'; and his awareness, finally, of
the importance of regional traditions and local skills all combined to make
him an early apostle of the modern neo-classical movement, still fashionable and flourishing today. An architect, decorator, designer and archivist,
he designed everything from furniture to ironwork, and from tapestry car-
toons to garden plans; his clientele, meanwhile, ranged from wealthy private
individuals to the Louvre, where he was responsible for refurbishing a number of galleries.

His own apartment contained a 'cabinet of curiosities' with, in each
corner, a piece of furniture devoted to the elements. Here he displayed
his accumulated minerals, fossils, shells and crystals, on shelves crowned
by pediments in the style of Borromini; his collection of 'eccentric
items', meanwhile, was disposed around a Renaissance
cabinet inlaid with polychrome marble. Finally, he
devoted a number of articles and studies to the subject
of cabinets of curiosities.

According to Moreux, three principal characteristics
distinguished the object of curiosity. Predictably, the

first of these is close to Surrealism: the 'effect of surprise as manifested by a more or less violent reaction in the face of the unexpected'.[65] For a rationalist such as Moreux, this surprise could not be reduced to a simple effect, a fleeting emotion, nor could it resolve itself: 'in almost spontaneous fashion, moreover, it stimulates the desire for knowledge. Add to this, finally, the fact that it distracts the eye and amuses the intellect in proportion to its rarity, and its tactile value is indisputable.'

'Tactile value': we should not be surprised by the degree of significance accorded by Moreux to this quality, the most basic and also the most superficial, to the extent that sensuality of form, a passion for the physical aspect of the object, its texture and design (particularly in objects from nature) was one of the essential givens of his creations. He designed a lamp around the whorl of a fossil, for instance, and used an outsize nautilus shell, carved in sanded or white-leaded oak, for a table leg and numerous other furniture designs.

'Desire for knowledge': for Moreux, this was rooted, in quasi-immediate fashion, in a sensitivity to natural objects, and in the musings prompted by their composition: 'a poppy seedhead, its integuments eroded by the elements so that only the bare structure remains, makes one think of a discarded diadem, tossed away by a sylph. A bird skeleton with only a few wing feathers and one eye still attached becomes a thing of nightmares. A geode of dioptase (a form of copper), with its myriad subtly interlocking and wondrously coloured crystals, is like a miniature version of one of the strange grottoes in the *Hypnerotomachia Polyphili*. A fossil may be the source of numerous images of familiar objects, but all of them distorted and as it were transposed: through the play of analogies, a trilobite may metamorphose into a Negro mask studded with outlandish designs; an ammonite out of context becomes the golden horn of Capricorn, fallen to earth from the Zodiac; and a nautilus shell sliced through presents the most tangible and moving depiction of the equation of a spiral of equal growth.'[66]

Two threads may be teased from this magnificently literary litany. The first is a Valéry-like fascination with the

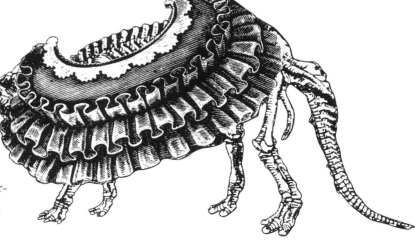

mathematical structure of natural objects, with the tension between the apparent irregularity of surfaces and the hidden code that underlies them. The second is the traditional theme of nature as creator of art, and of art serving and mirroring the wonders of nature ('since time immemorial, men have been struck by the shapes, colours and evocative powers of natural objects; hence they have made depictions of them with artistry, taking great care to render them accurately'): a dialectic of considerable significance, as we have seen, which in Moreux's approach becomes superimposed as a supplementary historical motif, adding to the shimmer of reminiscence perceptible behind every object.

His imagination seized by the concept of measurement, Moreux mingled the shells and minerals in his cabinet with an armillary sphere, a theodolite and a dodecahedron, marvellous creations which 'were admired not only as instruments specific to certain inquiries but also for their shapes and their intrinsic beauty',[67] and which presupposed an enhanced concern for matters of presentation. While 'De Laune and de Gourmont, Woeiriot and Boyvin, Bebam and de Bry designed and engraved admirable borders and cartouches, patterns in damascene, grotesqueries and Moorish motifs, encrusted with niello on both the framework and the support', Moreux was well aware that a cabinet of curiosities was as much a theatre of objects, and of exceptional objects, as a definition of a particular type of space: a space cut out and framed, encircled and embedded; a space in which one object nested within another, receding to infinity and opening up new spaces beyond number. This was a realm of envelopment, of which the extreme example, ultimate expression and focal point was the art of turning, which produced sheaths of wood or ivory turned in on themselves and enclosing only a central void. It was not by chance that Moreux dedicated the last months of his life to perfecting his designs for an exhibition at the Orangerie in Paris, in July 1956, devoted to 'cabinets of curiosities', in which, alongside natural curiosities, 'items of delicacy' (*pièces de délicatesse*) occupied a place of honour.

Château d'Oiron: the case of the Ichneumon

The various projects carried out from 1990 inside the Château d'Oiron, on the borders of Poitou and Val de Loire, offer some textbook studies in the authentic nature of cabinets of curiosities. Here – far from being viewed simply as a source of historical data, an influential motif or a frame of reference – the cabinet of curiosities is presented, literally and explicitly, as the very subject matter of art. Rejecting the historicist approach of reconstructing the original setting or interior, Jean Hubert Martin, who instigated the project, instead asked a number of contemporary artists of diverse nationalities to create, within the château, their own interpretation of the elements and spirit of the culture of curiosities ('the cabinet of curiosities', observes Martin, 'served in some way as an overall programme for the commissions').[68]

The point of departure and historical justification for the enterprise was provided by the presence within the château (which was rebuilt in the first half of the sixteenth century by Claude Gouffier, a distinguished military leader under François I) of a cabinet of curiosities. A few vestiges of this creation survived, scattered around the interior: a crocodile hanging on a wall, a pair of mongooses painted on *trompe-l'oeil* tablets, paintings on dappled marble, effigies of Roman emperors, and a mermaid-rabbit hybrid (probably a distorted version of a seal) within a painted emblem. These relics or allusions to items in the cabinet of curiosities thus offered themselves up, after a prolonged digression in time, for renewed processes of grafting and transplantation and an unexpected reinvention.

Surrounding these key elements are some of the themes that have emerged in earlier chapters of this work: the encyclopaedic ambitions of cabinets of curiosities; their striving towards an absolute knowledge, coupled with the futile nature of this endeavour; the dialectic between reason and magic; links with ancient bodies of knowledge; the rules (and the folly) of classification; fascination (through stones and fossilized shells) with the origins of life, and with sub- or superhuman creatures; distortions of scale, ranging from dwarves to giants; the dialectic between life and death; and finally and perhaps most tellingly, the inexhaustible force for creativity constituted by the errors and corollaries encountered in the quest for knowledge. This, in our view, represents the founding aesthetic principle of cabi-

It is possible to see the *Museum of Joseph Cornell* (1903–72) as a portable version, a reduction to the extreme, or the absurd, of the cabinet and its passion of enclosing one thing inside another – from furniture to shelves and from drawers to boxes.

nets of curiosities, the subtle convolutions of which have already been traced through the works of Sir Thomas Browne. The ichneumons or mongooses of the Château d'Oiron (or '*icnéfmons*', as they are described on the painted canvas) are emblematic here of all the hybrid creatures, deformities of nature and composite animals that clutter and illumine the history of cabinets of curiosities, including such exotica as unicorns, bezoars, mandragora and birds of paradise.

This was the starting point from which the project's creators proposed to 'draw viewers into a world of the imagination, to entice them into narratives involving role-plays and projection'.[69] The capacity to arouse wonder, which in the cabinet of curiosities was an essential attribute of any object belonging to the realms of the exotic or magic (while also stimulating the central passion – more or less overt – of the collector), here, in a further twist, becomes a speculative theme in every sense of the term. Clearly this is no longer a question of 'believing' in one virtue or secret property or another, or of pretending to do so, or even of half-pretending (like the eager collector tearing the claws off a bird of paradise that has arrived intact

CORNELL

The American Joseph Cornell (died 1972) is among the artists for whom the cabinet of curiosities proved a potent inspiration. He evolved a personal genre known as box assemblage, a form of three-dimensional collage, in which he sought to place elements as far apart from each other as possible, in the smallest possible space, thus creating multiple poetic resonances and provoking the spectator's capacity for association.

CHÂTEAU D'OIRON

The Château of Oiron, in central France, is a Renaissance house given up entirely to exercises in 20th- and 21st-century cabinets of curiosities, exploring every aspect of that genre and the way it can comment on contemporary culture. Its original builder was Claude Gouffier. The artist Guillaume Bijl's reconstruction (opposite) of that first cabinet, with the owner present as a waxwork, is at once a reflection on the impossibility of recapturing the past and on the irresistible desire to do so – which he sees as the impulse behind all collecting. It is also a criticism of mass tourism. The waxwork figure sums up all the ambiguities and ironies in such reconstructions: the décor surrounding it accumulates the emblems of a vanished culture while at the same time emptying them of meaning.

ABOVE Traditionally a Renaissance château would contain a portrait gallery of the owner's family and perhaps of royalty. Christian Boltanski's version (or perversion) of this feature is a collection of photographs of London schoolchildren.

because they contradicted its mythical status as the bird of eternal flight), but rather of inquiring into the roots, motives and mechanisms of such a desire; of revealing all that it conceals; and of pursuing in all its ramifications, however tenuous their connection, the interplay of amplifications, meanderings, inaccuracies, borrowings and inventions that feeds the world of wonders in all its manifestations.

Similarly, contemporary art now rediscovered, in a new application, the second founding theme of cabinets of curiosities: the division (and relationship) between art and the sciences, and between the skills of artists and of nature, in so doing reuniting borderline areas that had been separated by

Gouffier's Renaissance gallery at Oiron had included a series of portraits of giant men in armour between the windows, imitating a similar feature at Schloss Ambras. In their modern reincarnation by Daniel Spoerri (right) they have become three-dimensional assemblages following his *Warriors of the Night* (1981–85) and *Body in Pieces* (1990). Monstrous versions of the classical 'trophy', they are a mixture of artificial limbs, African masks, heads of wooden horses, a hippopotamus skull, tools and kitchen utensils. The fascination with waste and rubbish has antecedents in art, while the notion of assemblage opens the idea of the body as an organic whole to question, and beyond that the whole concept of unity and subjective identity.

history. As Martin remarks, 'the territory of art has been hugely enlarged by the inquiring approach of artists, who have laid claim to great swathes of the human and physical sciences in order to transpose or appropriate them for their own poetic ends'.[70] If the goal of the Château d'Oiron project, like that of many contemporary artists, is to return once more, and almost systematically, to the themes around which the history of cabinets of curiosities has developed, it does so at the price – or at the condition – of a no less methodical inversion of these motifs.

A journey such as this naturally finds one of its central motifs in the principle to which Lugli had already accorded a fundamental place in her analysis: the amassing of objects. It was an accumulation that lent itself to many different interpretations, the most immediate of which was sociological in nature, viewing the process as a parodic and critical reflection of the over-production and over-consumption that characterize western societies. But it was another, complementary aspect of the phenomenon that drew Martin's attention: the role of taste which, as we have seen, also ultimately played a decisive part in the history of cabinets of curiosities ('the accumulation of objects, dismissed as vulgar and popular by the age of classicism, has rediscovered its noble lineage as a convincing aesthetic phenomenon at the hands of numerous artists, the most widely known of whom is Arman').[71]

A critique of society or of taste: at a deeper level still, for Martin as for Lugli, the act of accumulation presented the ground for a critique of, or even a crisis in, aesthetics. While Lugli invoked the power of discontinuity, Martin focuses his attention on the celebration of the principle of 'heterogeneity', the juxtaposition of eclectic objects acting in his view, and in the eyes of the artists he has brought together, as a disruptive force that undermines not only the notions of 'unity' and the 'work', but also the concepts of the *auteur* and identity in general. From Beuys to Broodthaers and from Oldenburg to Boltanski, the line of descent from which the Château d'Oiron project draws its inspiration recalls that sketched out by Lugli, perhaps

For Oiron Thomas Grünfeld created a series of 'misfits', impossible animals that the classical lover of curiosities would have loved to collect. The 'Pegasus-Unicorn' (below) substitutes a buffalo horn for that of the narwhal, a customary object for cabinets, and a donkey with wings for Pegasus.

The *Crocodile of the Niger* by Mario Merz recreated in a quite unexpected way the element that was undoubtedly the most symbolic of the cabinet – the hanging crocodile – in the most distant, or the most real, context; the artificially low ceiling lit by neon.

according a special place to Spoerri, whose *Musée sentimental* (Centre Georges Pompidou, Paris, 1979) evoked strange resonances. In this work, according to Martin's description, 'he brought together relics and fetish objects from our history. Here, thrown together pell-mell, were Brancusi's nail clippers, Talleyrand's orthopaedic shoe, a casket containing locks of Victor Hugo's hair cut at different times of his life, a coffee spoon that belonged to Duchamp, Magritte's bowler hat, furniture from Van Gogh's bedroom in Auvers-sur-Oise, a suitcase that belonged to Rimbaud, a powder puff used to make up Paul McCartney, and – last but not least – Ingres' violin.'[72] A vertiginous reappearance, shifted across time, of Denon's reliquary, which itself stood as an emblematic summary of cabinets of curiosities in their golden age – with one single but fundamental reservation: that the (by definition) exceptional objects of the cabinets of curiosities are here present only as a ferocious and banal parody of themselves, the revolution (in values) here having turned full circle.

And this is not all. 'The artist', continues Martin, 'took care to offer a faithful description of the history of each object in a "little catalogue", thus following the traditional theme of the way the collector acquired, expanded and redefined his collection: he also laid stress on "the supporting value of a historical and fabulous chronicle assumed by the object"'. That which we have considered hitherto in terms of framing, appropriation and designation, at the Château d'Oiron passes through the realms of description, commentary and narrative, a process which simultaneously prolongs the life of the object, situates it, lends it depth, provides it with a (parodic) provenance or history and endows it with legitimacy. Another form of framing and appropriation and a new variation on the theme are provided by a scenario that is as historical as it phantasmagorical, and that invites every form of deviation, contamination and inaccuracy, in a systematic disruption of the historical data surrounding cabinets of curiosities. Around a waxwork figure, the artist

The cabinet reduced to a small cupboard, this work by Natasha Nicholson (born 1945) is above all a recepticle for a personal mythology.

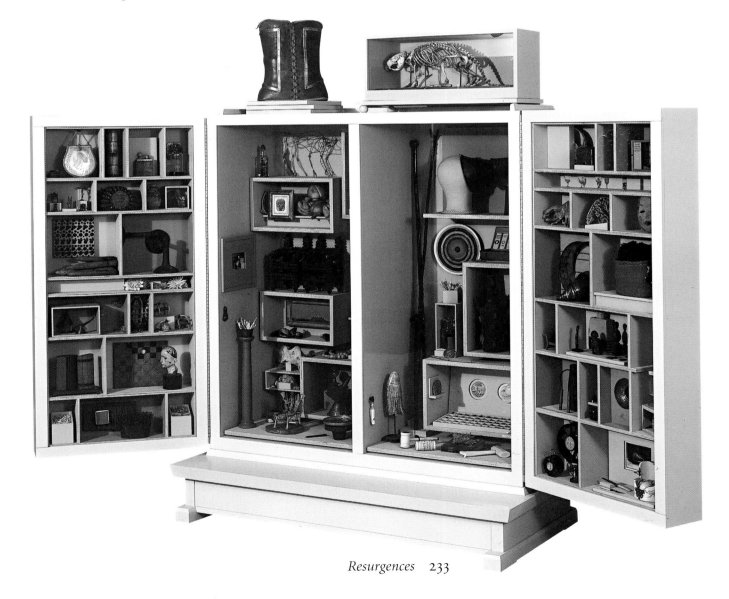

ANGEL

LELUM

HOMO

BRUTU

PLANTA

Guillaume Bijl 'reproduces the cabinet of Claude Gouffier, [...] with every element necessary for the re-creation of the image of this motley collection [...]: a serendipity of curious and bizarre objects, including stuffed animals, shells, scholarly works, scientific measuring instruments, weapons, etc. In his contribution, Thomas Grunfeld conjures up a menagerie of impossible hybrids, such as a 'Pegasus-Unicorn' with buffalo horns and swans' wings sprouting from the body of a donkey. Thomas Huber, meanwhile, offers a final disturbing vision of the multiplied cabinet of curiosities in the form of a dwarf as fetish object, after the manner of Aldrovandi or Rudolf II.[73] 'Objects,' he observes, 'the only remaining visible elements, are all that now remain of the shattered unity of being and appearance.'

The space of the discontinuous

Apart from the singular case of Moreux and the echo-games of the Surrealists, one has to wait until the last two decades of the twentieth century to witness the sudden and flamboyant reinvention of an object which had seemed to be definitively relegated to the margins of history and reserved for the lovers of dusty folios. In 1983 a handful of historians and other scholars from all over Europe converged on Oxford to celebrate the memory of Elias Ashmole, and thus brought back to life all the sleeping beauties from the history of the curiosity.[74] In that same year – a coincidence that provides one of the sources of and indeed the reasons for this present work – an Italian art historian, Adalgisa Lugli, published a large illustrated volume in which she took up the theme embarked on three quarters of a century earlier by Julius von Schlosser: in *Naturalia et Mirabilia* (Milan, 1983) she retraces the origins and offshoots of the curiosity, at the same time charting the course of this phenomenon during the sixteenth and seventeenth centuries. She was the harbinger of what has since been an unbroken series of publications and exhibitions devoted to the subject.

Lugli, who died in 1995, is doubly interesting in that she was at one and the same time an historian and an interpreter of the phenomenon – a sort of direct translator: barely three years after the publication of her book, she took part in the Second Venice Biennale, organizing an exhibition entitled *Wunderkammer,* which displayed a parallel montage of curiosities and contemporary works.

Like the artists gathered at the Chateau d'Oiron, the *Theatrum Mundi – Armarium* (*armarium* means a library cupboard) by Mark Dion makes explicit reference to the imaginary world of the cabinets of curiosities. Produced with the sculptor Robert Williams for an installation at Jesus College, Cambridge, in 2001, it also evokes the ideas of the Spanish mystic Ramond Lull. Lull saw the cosmos organized as follows: God, Angels, the Air, Humanity, Animals, Plants, Fire and Stones. Dion leaves God unimagined; Angels are represented by children's toys, videos, etc.; the Air by birds and butterflies; humanity by skulls and books; animals and plants by dried specimens.

For Lugli, the link with the Wunderkammer is forged by the fundamental importance of accumulation and collage in modern and contemporary art, its fascination with the heterogeneity of materials, and the importance attached to surroundings and conditions, to the 'environment' of the work, embedded as it is in a particular space. Paradoxically, the seemingly most extreme motifs of contemporary art – questioning the illusory unity of the visible, the coherence and division of space, the découpage and partitioning of forms and even of colours – these all hark back to the most archaic of forms and, just as one colour may 'awaken' another, they awaken the frameworks and the themes of cabinets of curiosity ('…if *ars combinatoria* and dislocation are two widespread processes in contemporary art, they nevertheless derive from a long creative tradition of love for the bizarre and the marvellous').[75]

Based on associations that are more or less arbitrary (in their appearance) and more or less justified (in their essence) – just as the cabinet of curiosities was based on analogy, correspondence or signature – the assemblage makes the artist into the same kind of furtive demiurge as the collector, as both seek to master the mysteries of nature. In giving himself over to creative liberty, to the dynamics of the unconscious, to the loss or the multiplication of identity, the modern artist bathes in the vaguely enchanted aura that once surrounded the collector. There is a symmetry here, for 'the collection has traditionally been the depository for a number of objects that cannot be homologized but are stored together in extremely audacious relationships. Most of the time, these associations have developed within the storehouses, and indeed in the very heart of the works themselves, giving rise to a rich variety of possible amalgamations'.[76] Thus the cabinet of curiosities contains potentially some of the basic ideas and driving forces of twentieth-century aesthetics. Indirectly, by accident, there has emerged the effect so essential for modern artists; space – the medium of contamination, the *locus* of chance encounters, the revealer of hidden meanings – this space, whose vital significance we have stressed again and again, once more emerges as the vital dimension, indeed the very principle underlying artistic creation.

Behind this latent correspondence between the assemblage and the cabinet of curiosities, Lugli sees an affirmation of the 'two major principles that govern relations between man and the world – the sense of continuity and that of discontinuity'.[77] In the enclosed world of the cabinet, it comes down – as we have seen – to interplay between micro and macro symmetries, to arrangements repeatedly fashioned along imaginary lines in order to establish a sense of continuity amid the disorder and discontinuity of reality, the chaos of the outside world. (Once again one must determine the collector's degree of consciousness of illusion, with respect to this continuity – a fascinatingly ambiguous subject for further study.) Similarly, the framed surface of the assemblage offers an affirmation of 'the sense of unity, of fusion between the objects, forms, figures and underlying foundations, and the possibility of making them interact and of extrapolating from the basis of these disparate fragments a composition that is perfectly unified'.[78]

A close friend of Jean Tinguely and Niki de Saint-Phalle, François-Xavier Lalanne (born in 1927) forms with his wife Claude one of the most singular couples in contemporary art. Famous for his animal sculptures which turn into something else (sheep-seats, rhinoceros-desk, ostrich-bracket), he imagined a series of eight 'objects of curiosity', entitled '*Flies' memory*'. Here a natural object, a fly, is transformed into art, and an art object, pottery, becomes through the passage of time, natural. A silver fly has settled on a Greco-Roman ointment jar, accentuating the *memento mori* aspect of the work (the monuments and pyramids collapse, the fly survives them).

Inside and outside the frame

'Arbitrarily' grouped together within set limits, the heterogeneous or 'discontinuous' objects of an assemblage confront the observer 'at the border of the indefinable': there is still perhaps a meaning that persists, but it is something fluid and ungraspable – the object, in all senses of the term, eludes the subject, defies his claims to comprehension, and confronts him with his own inability to latch on to things. For Lugli, this is another of those points of contact, or at least convergence, between the cabinet of curiosities and modern culture. There is no substantial gap between Dürer's *Melancolia* and a metaphysical interior by De Chirico: in both cases, a chaotic assembly of objects 'extends' a figure, or says what the figure cannot say, or effaces it, or supplants it, leaving nothing but a few traces. Correspondingly (in what binds him, as we have seen, to the culture of the emblem and the allegory, or to melancholic pathology), the collector of curiosities, fascinated by inanimate bodies and caught up in his own fascination, is ceaselessly threatened by 'contamination' brought about by his attraction to an immobility that runs contrary to 'life'. If, by seizing on a single aspect, he claims to have mastered the complexity of the whole and the infinite variety of reality, he will continually find himself challenged and overtaken by this complexity, and risks being literally lost in his fascination.

The tension between the parts and the whole, as seen in so many forms in the cabinet of curiosities, takes on its full polemic force in the modern assemblage. Ever questioning, deconstructing (or re-constructing) the notion of unity (that of the image as well as that of the viewer), it becomes an instru-

Considered one of the most important artists of his generation, Miquel Barceló (born in 1957) lives in his Parisian workshop surrounded by objects brought back from the other places where he has lived and worked, Majorca and Mali. Animal skulls, goat or fish heads, skeletons or carcasses found in Africa: all these left-overs, or waste, are the very objects of Barceló's painting, which is at the same time deeply impregnated with Mediterranean memories, themes and motives of ancient painting (and echoes of Twombly or Baroque artists).

ment of general dislocation. The cabinet was a matter of frames, and frames within frames; the assemblage, with its multiplicity of paradoxes, goes so far as to question even the possibility of regrouping, organizing, hierarchizing, partitioning and staging anything. The questions posed are an attack even on the function of the most rigid (though least substantial) of all the frames of a work – namely, its title: 'beyond the picture, the frame, and the collection of objects or situations assembled by the painting, the title establishes another frame: it is the supplementary container which leads us to seek places between the objects represented'.[79]

It is therefore the very provision of a title, a frame, a pointer that dramatizes the assemblage or collage, for it penetrates to the very foundations of the aesthetic act. After Duchamp, Dada and Surrealism, the mere isolation of an object became an *oeuvre* (the cabinet of curiosities, mixing objects of art and science, natural specimens and artefacts, posed a similar question concerning the quality, substance and place of the work of art in relation to

objects given in nature). Lugli insists on the central role of Surrealism, noting that 'before everything else, the found object is transported into the studio', where it takes on a new force while at the same time irradiating the things around it – the starting-point of a metamorphosis and of a game of infinite transformations. When Breton photographs 'accumulations and random assemblages on meat counters or in the streets of Paris', he is recognizing a work of art that is already there waiting to be revealed – that is to say, waiting to be given a title and a place.

If earlier we dwelt on the actual nature of the Surrealist object, and on what links it to the metaphorical and magical powers of the *Wunderkammer* object, now we shall consider this same object in situ: within the particular space of a room, a montage or a frame, which all offer just as many levels of reflection on and criticism of the classical concept of what constitutes a work of art. Among the complexities of the great Surrealist shows, the object itself was only one piece of the puzzle made up by the room or the entire exhibition, which was like a work that had exploded into multiple units. In this context, far from being a problematic accessory, 'photography plays a leading role here. It alone is an instrument capable of restoring a sense of the circularity, the totality and the indissoluble unity of space. In the sixteenth century,' Lugli reminds us, 'it is engraved reproductions that allow the gaze to take in the continuity extending to all points in the space of the *Wunderkammer*'.[80]

The apparatus of the Dadaists and the Surrealists thus initiates the process by which ultimately 'the box, the surroundings and the installation have definitively replaced the picture-frame.' Photographs of exhibitions – by their nature, temporary events – or of ephemeral installations, act as a sort of symmetrical counterpart to the engraved frontispiece which fixed for ever the meticulous and stimulating order of the curiosities.

In this evolution towards the transformation of space into a genuine aesthetic fact, the cabinet of curiosities offers to a number of artists the image of a kind of 'primal scene' of their own work: it is a place where one finds the premises of what will later become the modern 'museum', where original desires have not yet been trammelled by institutions, and where rules are established for the appreciation of objects. The object in

Françoise de Nobèle was among the first to adopt the cabinet of curiosities as a source of inspiration for ordinary décor. An antiques dealer and collector, she had grown up in a world of magic spells, ancient books and old engravings, leading her to develop a highly personal '*sentiment visuel*'. In her apartment one finds popular souvenirs, examples of modern art, and theatre and garden chairs, side by side with stuffed animals, the mummy of an Egyptian cat and classical furniture.

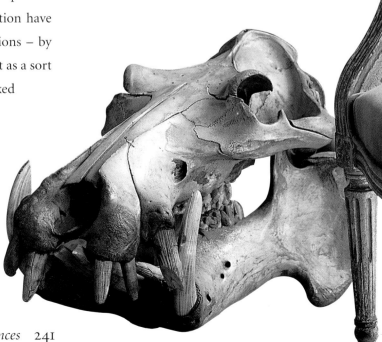

Characteristics of Françoise de Nobèle's décor are the papier-mâché animals and plants made as teaching aids by the firm of Auzoux in the first half of the 20th century, remarkable for the finesse of their execution and the tactile qualities of their materials; deprived of their didactic purpose they make their effect as works of art, fascinating in their disproportion of scale and their paradoxical poetry. Nothing in the aesthetic represented by these interiors can be said to be without significance, from the smallest nuances of colour (an extremely refined palette of greens, blacks and greys) to the textures of the rubbed, grated, and flaked surfaces. They represent an incomparable example of the 'faded' aesthetic, typical of a whole aspect of contemporary taste.

the cabinet originally offered a metaphor for the unknown, for something different, defined by multiple aspects, but now it has been transformed into a metaphor for enterprise, for the artistic gesture *per se*. It is an emblem of an emblem, creating one of those effects of multiplication which have always permeated the history of the *Wunderkammer*. All the artists – from Duchamp to Paolo Tessari, from Cornell to Messager, from Beuys to Spoerri – take as their subject-matter the conditions of exhibition, multiplying, deforming or varying them according to every possible form of rhetoric. Cases, glass cabinets, boxes, reliquaries – all those elements whose fundamental importance we have seen in both the history and the economics of curiosity – are now like fetishes, ironic or disenchanted forms, undefinable objects, distorted reflections which themselves reflect the status of

the work of art: the moment at which the work dissolves and disappears into its traditional definition is the moment at which, like a phantom, its first incarnation springs back into life.

'A slight slippage'

One of the consequences of the disappearance of the concept of the work, in the classical sense of the term, from modern and contemporary art has been the acceptance and recognition of realms and endeavours that have hitherto been excluded from the main body of art, or consigned to the fringes of the pathological. 'Natural poetry', dandies dabbling in extravagance and excess, Art Brut or Outsider Art: we are surrounded now by works without artists, or in which the vestiges of a consciousness or an identity have vanished, and artists without works, whose only legacy is their lives, or even some device, place or mere intention. As an accumulation of objects, a theatre of intimacy, a fundamentally eclectic assortment of objects, the cabinet of curiosities belongs as we have seen, under numerous different guises and via a number of essential connections, to the history of modern and contemporary art. But the closing years of the twentieth century witnessed the emergence of a final renaissance, as spectacular as it was unexpected, of the *Wunderkammern*, in a resurgence that took place, moreover, outside the confines of any cultural establishment, no matter how cutting-edge or controversial. Quite the reverse: a côterie of collectors and cognoscenti now chose, quietly and in private, to adopt the vanished cabinets of curiosities as the décor against which they lived their daily lives, creating spaces saturated with references and allusions, rêveries around themes and objects long ago consigned to oblivion, the carefully meditated frameworks of a personal scenography which to the astute observer will appear as so many works without titles, paradoxical testimonies of daily life in the era of new technology.

What are we to make, for example, of the cabinet of wonders created by David Hildebrand Wilson in a western suburb of Los Angeles? Sandwiched between a carpet store and a real estate office, with a forensics lab and a Thai restaurant as its neighbours, this small and unassuming building, which its owner has glorified, disconcertingly, with the title of Museum of Jurassic Technology, is entered through a doorway flanked by a pair of bizarre, rudimentary dioramas, presenting on one side a tableau of 'a diminutive white urn surrounded by floating pearlescent moths', and on the other 'three chemistry-set bottles arrayed in a curious loving display'.[81]

Although the avowed and rather puzzling aim of this work is the 'appreciation of the late Jurassic' (Wilson's wife professes a distinct penchant for his 'Neanderthal appearance'), it quickly becomes clear that it falls into another, quite different category. Here are some of the objects on display there, among other *mirabilia*: the skeleton of a mole on a velvet ground; a collection of 'now-extinct nineteenth-century French moths'; a model of Noah's Ark mounted on two pistons that move; a succession of horns and antlers, including a horn of hair taken from the head of one Mary Davies, who died in 1688, aged seventy-one, at Saughall in Cheshire; a wax hand clutching a bird, the embodiment of the Platonic image of the memory; a small black onyx box used to hold sacrificed human hearts; thirty needles, the eyes of which contain micro-miniature sculptures (Pope John Paul II, Snow White, etc.) a fruit stone carving featuring, in a space measuring thirteen millimetres by eleven, a Flemish landscape, a bearded viol player, a bear, an elephant, a dog, a monkey, a camel, a lynx, rabbits and an owl and on the back a Crucfixion with a soldier on horseback; a wish ('may all your dreams come true') engraved on a hair; and finally a collection of correspondence sent to the Mount Wilson Observatory between 1915 and 1935, containing one letter asserting that the Earth is flat and motionless, another proposing a voyage to Mars, and a third claiming that its signatory had turned silver into gold for the American government.

In other words, the space presents all the distinguishing marks of a museum, albeit a slightly impoverished one, hard up and improvised, put together in *ad hoc* fashion by a collector tinged with fanaticism and not wholly equipped to realize his ambitions. One becomes dimly aware, as a perceptive visitor has observed, 'that something is wrong. There is a very slight slippage which is the very essence of the place.'[82] Slippage, shifting, displacement, a slight – if not rather disturbing – feeling of strangeness: all so many notes on the sliding scale of emotions associated with the culture of curiosities, here presented in a marginally different key and a wholly incongruous setting.

This visitor goes further: Wilson's cabinet, he notes, 'deploys all the traditional signs of a museum's institutional authority – meticulous presentation, exhaustive captions, hushed lighting, and state-of-the-art

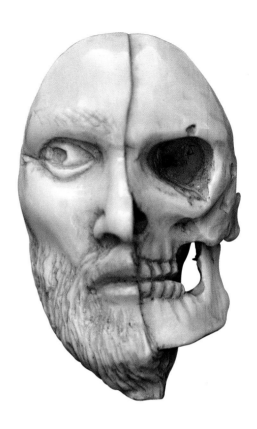

Solange Fouilleul is another Parisian collector who continues the tradition of the cabinet of curiosities. A dominant theme is *vanitas* or *memento mori* and her apartment is haunted by skulls and skeletons of every form and from every culture.
OPPOSITE (BACKGROUND) One of a group of 19th-century Japanese skeleton musicians made of metal.
ABOVE Life and death, a French 19th-century ivory divided into face and skull.

Another room in Solange
Fouilleul's apartment is devoted
exclusively to books and objects
in cupboards and chests of
drawers. In the showcase
(opposite) are shells and minerals;
next to it a 19th-century globe
with above it a 19th-century
trompe l'oeil watercolour and
a portrait composed of shells
in the manner of Arcimbaldo.

technical armature – all to subvert the very notion of the authoritative as it applies not only to himself but to any museum'.[83] Naive or knowing, just like the cabinets of curiosities of history, Wilson's becomes a *de facto* ready-made in the manner of Duchamp, an inscrutable statement and performance piece that can claim its place as a work of art alongside the most complex of installations.

In returning to some of the fetish objects of early cabinets of curiosities (a hair horn formed part of the collection of Elias Ashmole in around 1650, for instance, and the history of curiosities is littered with references to

engraved cherry stones and other miniature carvings), Wilson seeks above all to rekindle the basic emotion that is stimulated, in Weschler's summary, by the contemplation of otherness, the sense of wonder that has found new expression in this out-of-the-way part of Los Angeles, and that 'stands for all that cannot be understood, that can scarcely be believed. It calls attention to the problem of credibility, and at the same time insists upon the undeniability, the exigency of experience.'[84] And it is an experience in which we cannot fail to recognize that of the culture of curiosities.

But according to the rules of the genre, Wilson's cabinet would be nothing without its catalogue: a catalogue which here unusually takes the form not of an inventory drawn up by the collector or an accomplice, but rather of an intriguing work, lying somewhere between narrative chronicle and fiction, penned by a simple visitor who found himself disconcerted by the spirit of the place. Indeed, in his *Mr Wilson's Cabinet of Wonder* (New York, 1995) Lawrence Weschler offers not only a description of the place and insights into its intentions, but also a strange, dogged blend of fantasy and serious endeavour, reflecting and multiplying the naïve sophistication, the intermingling of myth and science, of knowledge and belief that are inherent in

One of the few British collectors is Alistair McAlpine, a man of varied occupations and talents, who has turned his antiques shop into a cabinet of curiosities. In the great tradition, he is fascinated by everything – classical sculpture, Australian minerals, a dinosaur egg, stone-age flints, Egyptian canopic jars, a dried crocodile…. There is no theme to his collection, and he lives with it as part of his daily existence.

Wilson's enterprise; and this reflection is distorted in turn by the heterogeneous mixture, hesitating between one definition and another, that was essential to historical cabinets of curiosities. With its invocation borrowed from Borges and its embracing of the principle according to which erudition is the modern form of the fantastical, Weschler's 'catalogue' multiplies, apparently *ad libidum*, the plays on slippage and shifting, and of objects-within-objects, that are present in explicit fashion, to a greater or lesser degree, in the history of cabinets of curiosities. The author became aware of these plays of infinite resonance and random fault lines only upon reading an inspired work, now unavailable: Impey and MacGregor's edition of papers presented at a conference in 1983 on the subject of the Ashmolean and collections of curiosities. A final, and provisional, divagation in the rambling, many-branched genealogy of the culture of curiosities.

Mosaic and Missing Pieces

Occasionally open to visitors but expecting more to be stumbled upon by those who have lost their way, Wilson's cabinet – in order to play the part of its alibi, its 'museum-fiction' – is a semi-public space. It forms part of a handful of domestic spaces and private interiors scattered throughout different regions and countries at the end of the twentieth century, in which the culture of curiosities serves as an everyday reference, offering a selection of objects and models as well as a specific organization of space. Despite Poe's *Philosophy of Furniture* and Praz's *Filosofia dell' arredamento*, general culture does not yet consider these 'interior arrangements' as works of art, whether or not they are linked to the name of a particular artist. Yet – carefully considered and deliberated over as they are – these constructions (both physical and mental), artefacts and installations carry their own meaning, and we should delay no further in according them a significance that goes beyond their simple historical or sociological status.

These works are by their nature ephemeral or even invisible, as Breton's office wall would have been had it not been saved and re-erected in the context of a museum. And their very impermanence increases the power of their fascination. For what force, theme or common interest could bring together – without any of them having the slightest notion of it – a Paris bookshop, a prominent Londoner, an expert in vanities and an illustrator living a secluded life in the English countryside? They are all collectors, of course, and in varying degrees their interiors all display not only a concern and love for objects, but also and more crucially objects that are now out of place, stripped of both function and meaning by the march of reason and history; objects that are substantially obsolete and out of their time, and that are suddenly offered an abrupt and paradoxical renaissance. Here we find again Walter Benjamin's vision of the collector as a being within whom childish attributes – notably delight and enchantment at the acquisition and handling of a book or other object which is thus itself renewed – meld seamlessly with the venerable, dusty exterior of an antiquary.[85] After their own fashion, therefore, collectors such as these take up again, and produce new variations upon, the theme of the *senex puerilis* which belongs so wholeheartedly to the history of the culture of curiosities.

These remarkable accumulations of objects also share another unmistakable characteristic: a taste for particular substances, colours and textures, a heightened awareness of tactile qualities, and a broad palette of rare and unusual forms and materials. The dry and varnished surface of dense materials, the grainy sleekness of *papier mâché*, the nut-brown patina of bones, the austere monochrome patterns of faded fabrics, the counterpoint of coral and ivory, the raw power of ethnographical objects contrasted with the finesse of waxworks and plaster casts: these are their common currency. And these hieratic arrangements set within open cabinets, like so many altars or offertories, these display cases and drawers, these compartments laid out with painstaking care, all retranscribe in their own way the naïve symmetries of the early cabinets of curiosities.

This importance accorded to tactile qualities is a message in itself. It defies and stands in opposition to the graphic tones, fluid, flashing and reflective, of modern scientific images, consecrated wholly to the demands of computer screen technology and virtual reality. Similarly, the pure unblemished surfaces and intangible seams of the products of modern manufacturing technology find their antithesis in the fragmented surfaces of bones and bodies, the dusty crevices of stuffed animals, and all that is essentially approximate and improvised in this reconstructed universe.

What was highlighted by these interiors was not so much the relationship between *artificialia* and *naturalia*, and between science and art, as that between a body of scientific knowledge that was already dated, obsolete and infused with nostalgia and memories (as epitomized by objects used in

In a suburb of Los Angeles, David Hildebrand Wilson's 'Museum of Jurassic Technology' seems like the ultimate parody of the cabinet of curiosities. A baffling mixture of the genuine and the bogus, it recaptures the sense of arcane knowledge, folk-beliefs and the feeling that the world is a more peculiar place than one suspected. One of its exhibits is a 'human horn', sawn off the head of a 70-year-old woman in the middle of the 19th century. By way of explanation this 17th-century engraving is shown of Mary Davis of Saughall in Cheshire: 'When she was 28 years old she had an excrescence upon her head which continued 32 years like a wenn; then grew into two horns; after three years she cast them. These upon her head have grown four years and are loose.'

early schoolrooms) and an artistic consciousness that was by contrast highly advanced, informed and exacting. And behind the poetics of rejects and relics that run like a common thread through these compositions, there looms – as to a greater or lesser degree throughout the history of cabinets of curiosities – the contrast and dialectic between 'noble' and 'inferior' forms of knowledge, a desire for the re-evaluation and rehabilitation of these objects to which (from ethnographical items to examples of popular art) scant respect had hitherto been accorded. Thus in their own fashion these interiors champion a deep-rooted freedom of appreciation, in the authentic sense of the term: they seek to give worth to that which before was dismissed as worthless.

A passion for rejects and relics is also, taken from another point of view, a fascination with fragments, and particularly with fragments of the body, the most fundamental image of the 'whole'. And just as they stand in contrast to the 'virtual image', so these interiors celebrate, in innumerable different forms but most obviously through bones and skeletons, the image of the imperfection of humanity in its bodily forms, as opposed to the cosmetically flawless, marble-smooth, never-fading bodily perfection that dominates the imagination of modern societies. Their focus is the body-as-mechanism, a paradoxical body that can be dismantled, the internal workings of which may be brought to the surface and endlessly elaborated, with detailed studies of individual aspects such as the architecture of the skeleton, the network of veins and veinlets, the arborescence of the arterial system, the muscular sheath, the iridescent tissues, the vitreous humours, and the contours of the bones. A wonderful assemblage indeed, yet its most wondrous feature lies in its essential fragility, its constant readiness to fall into decay, to become a mere farrago of morsels and fragments.

The images presented in these pages, and the accompanying themes taken from texts, fragments and pictures over the years and disposed here in a semblance of order, may we hope offer new and (as ever) transitory insights into this fragmentary jigsaw, or – to return to a metaphor that forms a leitmotif throughout the history of cabinets of curiosities – this mosaic with missing pieces.

Notes

1 See G. Olmi, *Tous les savoirs du monde*, Paris, 1996, p. 160.
2 See Adalgisa Lugli, *Naturalia et Mirabilia: Il collezionismo enciclopedico nelle Wunderkammern d'Europa*, Milan, 1990, p. 43.
3 Quoted by G. Olmi, *op. cit.*, p. 275.
4 See Michael Hunter, *Elias Ashmole and His World*, Oxford, 1983, p. 13
5 G. Olmi, *op. cit.*, p. 273.
6 An exemplary study of the iconographic and symbolic links in the circle of Francesco I de' Medici can be found in Luciano Berti, *Il principe dello Studiolo*, Florence, 1967.
7 Quoted by G. Olmi, 'Science, honour, metaphor' in Impey and MacGregor, *The Origins of Museums: the Cabinet of Curiosities in Sixteenth- and Seventeenth-Century Europe*, Oxford, 1985. See also A. A. Shelton, 'Cabinets of transgression' in Elsner and Cardinal, *The Cultures of Collecting*, London, 1994.
8 A. A. Shelton, 'Renaissance collections and the new world' in Elsner and Cardinal, *op. cit.* See also Laura Laurencich Minelli, in Impey and MacGregor, *op. cit.*, pp. 18–22.
9 See text by Thomas Da Costa Kauffman in E. Irblich, *Le Bestiaire de Rodolphe II*, Paris, 1990, and *The Mastery of Nature*, Princeton, 1993.
10 See L. Daston and K. Park, *Wonders and the Order of Nature 1150–1750*, New York, 1998, p. 255.
11 L. Daston and K. Park, *op. cit.*, p. 258.
12 See J. Kenseth (ed.), *The Age of the Marvelous*, Hanover, New Hampshire, 1991, p. 87.
13 G. Olmi, *op. cit.*, p. 275.
14 L. Daston and K. Park, *op. cit.*, p. 275.
15 *Ibid.*, p. 288.
16 Jean de Heem, quoted by L. Daston and K. Park, *op. cit.*, p. 284.
17 L. Daston and K. Park, *op. cit.*, p. 328.
18 Walter Benjamin, *Je déballe ma bibliothèque…*
19 Michael Hunter, *op. cit.*, p. 18.
20 Lytton Strachey, 'John Aubrey', in *Biographical Essays*, London, 1948.
21 *Cf.* G. Olmi, 'Italian Cabinets of the Sixteenth and Seventeenth centuries', in O. Impey and A. MacGregor, *op. cit.*, p. 5
22 G. Olmi, *op. cit.*, p. 292 and Kenseth, *op. cit.*, note 108.
23 L. Laurencich Minelli, 'Museography and ethnographical…' in O. Impey and A. MacGregor, *op. cit.*, p. 20.
24 See Kenseth, *op. cit.*, note 108.
25 G. Olmi, 'Italian Cabinets…', *art. cit.*, p. 8.
26 *Ibid.*, p. 10.
27 Kenseth, *op. cit.*, note 14, p. 234.
28 See catalogue *I segreti di un collezionista. Le straordinaire zaccolte di cassiano del Pozzo*, Rome, 2000, pp. 37–38.
29 Kenseth, *op. cit.*, note 16, p. 237.
30 *Ibid.*, p. 238 and Laura Laurencich Minelli, *art. cit.*, pp. 17–19.
31 L. L. Minelli, *art. cit.*, p. 19.
32 G. Olmi, 'Italian Cabinets…', p. 11.
33 *Ibid.*, p. 12.
34 See G. Olmi, *op. cit.*, p. 295.
35 O. Impey and A. MacGregor, *op. cit.*, p. 26.
36 G. Olmi, *op. cit.*, p. 12.
37 See Kenseth, *op. cit.*, p. 242.
38 John Evelyn, *Diary*, (ed. W. Bray), London, 1907 and 1914, November 1644.
39 See *Athanasius Kircher: Il Museo del Mondo*, Rome, 2001.
40 See Kenseth, *op. cit.*, p. 242.
41 Herbert Haupt, in E. Irblich, *op. cit.*

42 W. Muensterberger, *Collecting, an Unruly Passion*, Princeton, 1994, pp. 16 and 193.
43 Sir Thomas Browne, *Pseudodoxia Epidemica*, I, XXI, ed. Robin Robbins, Oxford and New York, 1981.
44 See G. Olmi, *op. cit.*, p. 266.
45 Marianne Roland-Michel, *Lajoue*, Paris, 1984, pp. 42 and 44–45.
46 Marianne Roland-Michel, *op.cit*, pp. 44–45 and 186–87.
47–50 L. Daston and K. Park, *op. cit*, pp. 331, 343, 354, 366.
51 See the catalogue of the exhibition at the Louvre (*Dominique Vivant Denon, L'Œil de Napoléon*, RMN, 1999), edited by Patrick Mauriès (*Vies remarquables de Vivant Denon*, 1998), and Philippe Sollers, *Le Cavalier du Louvre*, Paris, 1995.
52 I. Amin Ghali, quoted by Patrick Mauriès, *op. cit.* p. 88.
53 *Catalogue de la vente Denon*, n°346, Paris, 1826 (quoted in Mauriès, *op. cit.*, pp. 89–90).
54 See Mauriès, *op. cit*, pp. 418, 421.
55 See E. H. Gombrich, *Aby Warburg, an Intellectual Biography*, London, 1970, pp. 243–255.
56 All the quotations on the subject of Meyrick are taken from the chapter devoted to him in Clive Wainwright's *The Romantic Interior*, London and New Haven, 1989, pp. 241–268.
57 H. R. D'Allemagne, *Les Cartes à jouer du XIVe au XXe siècle*, Paris, 1906.
58 H. R. D'Allemagne, *Histoire des jouets*, Paris, 1880 and 1902; *Jeux du jeune âge*, Paris 1908; *Musée Rétrospectif de la classe 100, jouets, à l'Exposition Universelle*, Paris, 1903; *Histoire du luminaire depuis l'époque romaine jusqu'au XIXe siècle*, Paris, 1891.
59 H. R. D'Allemagne, *Les Accessoires du costume et du mobilier depuis le treizième jusqu'au milieu du dix-neuvième siècle*, Paris, 1928.
60 A. Breton, *Objets surréalistes, Œuvres complètes*, Paris.
61 A. Breton, *Situation surréaliste de l'objet*, 1935, *Œuvres complètes*, t. 2, Paris, p. 473.
62 A. Breton, *De l'humour noir*, Paris, 1937.
63 A. Breton, *Situation surréaliste de l'objet*, *op. cit.*, p. 495.
64 A. Breton, *Situation surréaliste de l'objet*, *op. cit.*, p. 492.
65 Jean-Charles Moreux, 'L'Objet de curiosité', *Maison et Jardin*, 20, 1954, p. 81.
66 Jean-Charles Moreux, *op. cit.*, p. 80.
67 Jean-Charles Moreux, 'Le Cabinet du curieux', *Art et Industrie*, Juin 1950, p. 17.
68 Jean Hubert Martin, *Le Château d'Oiron et son cabinet de curiosités*, Paris, 2000, p. 64.
69–73 J. H. Martin, *op. cit.*, p. 126, 134, 136, 246, 262.
74 The translation of this conference can be found in O. Impey and A. MacGregor, *op. cit.*
75 Adalgisa Lugli, *Assemblage*, Paris, 2001, p. 32.
76–80 A. Lugli, *op. cit.*, pp. 32, 27, 28, 43, 88.
81–83 Lawrence Weschler, *Mr Wilson's Cabinet of Wonder*, New York, 1995, pp. 121, 39, 40.
84 Stephen Greenblatt quoted by Weschler, *op. cit.*, p. 79.
85 (See above, pp. 134–5.)

Select Bibliography

Original Sources

Descrizione del Museo d'Antiquaria e del Gabinetto d'Istoria Naturale di sua Eccelenza il Sig. Principe di Biscari Ignazio Paterno Castello Patrizio Catanese Fatta dall'Abate Domenico Sestini, 1776.

Catalogue raisonné d'une collection considérable de diverses Curiosités en tous genres, contenues dans les cabinets de feu Monsieur Bonnier de la Mosson, Edme-François Gersaint, Paris, J. Barois et P.-G. Simon, 1744.

Les Antiquitez, raretez, plantes, mineraux, & autres choses considérables de la Ville, & Comté de Castres d'Albigeois…. Et un recueil des inscriptions romaines, & autres antiquitez du Languedoc, & Provence. Avec le Roole des principaux cabinets, & autres raretez de l'Europe. Comme aussi le Catalogue des choses rares de Maistre Pierre Borel, Docteur en Medecine autheur de ce livre, Pierre Borel, Castres, Arnaud Colomiez, 1649.

Certain miscellany tracts. Written by Thomas Browne, Kt, and Doctour of Physick, Thomas Browne, London, printed for Ch. Mearne and sold by Henry Bonwick, 1684.

Ricreatione dell'occhio e della mente nell'Osservation' delle Chioccole, proposta a' Curiosi delle Opere della Natura, Filippo Buonanni, Rome, Varese, 1681.

Musaeum Franc. Calceolari Iun. Veronensis a Benedicto Ceruto medico in caeptum, et ab Andrea Chiocco descriptum et perfectum, Francesco Calzolari, Verone, Angelus, Tamus, 1622.

Museo Cospiano annesso a quello del famoso Ulisse Aldrovandi e donato alla sua Patria dal'Illustrissimo Signor Ferdinando Cospi, Bologne, Giacomo Monti, 1677.

Description des Objets d'art qui composent le Cabinet de feu M. le Baron Vivant Denon. Estampes et ouvrages à figure, Duchesne l'aîné, Paris, printed by Hippolyte Tilliard, 1826.

Catalogue raisonné des Tableaux, Estampes, Coquilles, et autres Curiosités; après le décès de feu Monsieur Dezalier d'Argenville, Pierre Rémy, Paris, chez Didot l'aîné, 1766.

Catalogue des tableaux de la Galerie Electorale à Dresde, J. A. Riedel and C. F. Wenzel, Dresden, printed by Chrétien-Henri Hagemuller, 1765.

Le Cabinet de la Bibliothèque de Sainte Geneviève, Claude Du Molinet, Paris, chez Antoine Dezallier, 1692.

Catalogue raisonné des minéraux, coquilles et autres curiosités naturelles, contenues dans le cabinet de feu Mr. Geoffroy de l'Académie des Sciences, Paris, H.-L. Guérin et L.-Fr. Delatour, 1753.

Catalogue raisonné de coquilles et autres curiosités naturelles avec une liste des principaux Cabinets qui s'en trouvent, tant dans la France que dans la Hollande, Edme-François Gersaint, Paris, Flahault, Prault, 1736.

Dell'Historia naturale nella quale ordinatamente si tratta della diversa condition di miniere e pietre. Con alcune historie di Piante & Animali, fin'hora non date in luce, Naples, Costantino Vitale, 1599.

Obeliscus Pamphilius hoc est, interpretatio obelisci hieroglyphici, Athanasius Kircher, Rome, Louis Grignani, 1650.

Ars magna sciendi in XII libros digesta, Athanasius Kircher, Amsterdam, Jean Jansson, 1669.

Musaeum Kircherianum, sive Museaum a P. Athan. Kirchero… nuper restitum, auctum, descriptum & iconibus illustratum Franc. Maria Ruspolo oblatum a Ph. Bonanni, Filippo Buonanni, Rome, Georgio Plachi, 1709.

Catalogue raisonné des différents objets de curiosités dans les sciences et arts, qui composaient le Cabinet de feu Mr Mariette, F. Basan, Paris, the author and G. Desprez, 1775.

Note overo Memorie del Muso di Lodovico Moscardo nobile veronese, Padua, Paolo Frambotto, 1656.

L'Art de tourner ou de faire en perfection toutes sortes d'ouvrages au tour, dans lequel on y enseigne pour tourner tant le bois, l'ivoire etc. que le fer et tous les métaux, Charles Plumier, Lyon, Jean Certe, 1701.

Description abrégée des planches, qui représentent les cabinets et quelques-unes des Curiosités, contenües dans le Théâtre des Merveilles de la Nature de Levin Vincent, Romain de Hooghe et alii, Harlem, 1719.

Museum Wormianum. Seu Historia rerum rariorum, tam naturalium, quam artificialium, tam domesticarum, quam exoticarum, quae Hafniae Danorum in aedibus authoris servantur, Olao Worm, Leiden, J. Elzevir, 1655.

Sources of illustrations

Modern Works

Athanasius Kircher: Il Museo del Mondo, Rome, 2001.

Bergvelt, Elinor, Debora J. Mieijers, Mieke Rijnders, *Verzamelen ven Raiteitenkabinet tot Kunstmuseum*, Heerlen, 1993.

Daston, Lorraine and Katharine Park, *Wonders and the Order of Nature 1150–1750*, New York, 1998.

Elsner, John and Roger Cardinal (ed.), *The Cultures of Collecting*, London, 1994.

Erasme ou l'éloge de la curiosité à la Renaissance: Cabinets de curiosités et jardins de simples, Brussels, 1997.

Habsburg, Géza von, *Princely Treasures*, London, 1997.

Impey, Oliver and Arthur MacGregor, *The Origins of Museums: The Cabinet of Curiosities in Sixteenth- and Seventeenth-Century Europe*, Oxford, 1985.

Kaufmann, Thomas Da Costa, *The Mastery of Nature*, Princeton, 1993.

Kenseth, Joy, *The Age of the Marvelous*, Hanover, 1991.

Lugli, Adalgisa, *Arte e Scienza: Wunderkammer*, Venice, 1986.

Lugli, Adalgisa, *Naturalia e mirabilia*, Milan, 1983.

Lugli, Adalgisa, *Wunderkammer: la stanza della meraviglia*, Turin, 1997.

Lugli, Adalgisa, *Assemblage*, ed. Florian Rodani, Paris, 2001.

Martin, Jean Hubert, *Le Château d'Oiron et son cabinet de curiosités*, Paris, 2000.

McAlpine, Alistair and Cathy Giangrande, *Collecting and Display*, London, 1998.

Müller-Bahlke, Thomas J., *Die Wunderkammer: die Kunst- und Naturalien Kammer der Franckeschen Stiftungen zu Halle*, Photographs by Klaus E. Göltz, Halle/Saale, 1998.

Olmi, G., *Tous les savoirs du monde*, Bibliothèque nationale, Paris, 1996.

I Segreti di un Collezionista: le straordinarie raccolte di Cassiano dal Pozzo 1588–1657, Rome, 2000.

Somino, Annalisa Scarpa, *Cabinet d'amateur: le Grandi Collezioni d'Arte nei Dipinti dal XVII al XIX Secolo*, Milan, 1992.

Le surréalisme: sources – histoire – affinités, Paris, 1965.

Thornton, Dora, *The Scholar in his Study*, New Haven, 1997.

Weschler, Lawrence, *Mr Wilson's Cabinet of Wonder*, New York, 1995.

Abbreviations:
BL – British Library, London
BM – British Museum, London
FS – Franckeschen Stiftungen, Halle
GG – Grünes Gewölbe, Dresden
KHM – Kunsthistorisches Museum, Vienna
SA – Schloss Ambras

page 1 Museo dell' Opificio delle Pietre Dure, Florence. Photo: Scala 2–3 Photo: Jean Marie Del Moral 4 ostrich made from a misshapen pearl, Museo degli Argenti, Florence. Photo: Scala 4–5 cup made from nautilus shell, Antwerp, c. 1560, Landesmuseum, Kassel 5 Engraving from Christoph Jamnitzer, *Neuw Grottesken Buch*, Nuremberg, 1610 6–7 Engraving from M. Félibien, *Historie de l'Abbaye de Saint Denys*, Paris, 1706 8–9 Jan Brueghel and Peter Paul Rubens, *The Sense of Sight*, Museo del Prado, Madrid. Photo: Bridgeman 10–11 Ferrante Imperato, *Dell'historia naturale* (Naples, 1599) 10 (**bottom**) woodcut from Ferrante Imperato, *Dell'historia naturale* (Naples, 1599) 12 Francis Bacon, *Instauratia Magna*, 1620 12 (**background**) gilt bronze dolphin, Medici Collection, late sixteenth century. Photo: Scala 13 *studiolo* of Francesco I. Photo: Scala 13 (**left**) woodcut from Ferrante Imperato, *Dell'historia naturale* (Naples, 1599) 14–15 Francesco Calzolari, *Museum Calceolarium* (Verona, 1622), BL 16–17 drawing by Michael Kerr (1591–1661), University Library, Erlangen 18 engraved title-page of *Museum Wormianum* (Leyden, 1655) 20 woodcut from Ferrante Imperato, *Dell'historia naturale* (Naples, 1599) 21 engraving from the German edition of Edward Brown, *Travels* (Nuremberg, 1686), BL 22 title-page of Basilus Besler, *Fasciculus rariorum varii generis* (Nuremberg, 1622). Photo: BL 23 engraving from *Fasciculus rariorum varii generis* (Nuremberg, 1622) 24 woodcut from Conrad Gesner, *Thierbuch* (Zurich, 1563) 25 woodcut from Ferrante Imperato, *Dell'historia naturale* (Naples, 1599) 26–31 FS. Photos: Klaus E. Göltz 32–33 watercolour by Joseph Arnold (1646–74), Historical Museum, Ulm 34 painting from the ceiling of the dining-room, SA 35 Venetian mirror, late sixteenth century, SA. Photo: KHM 36–37 painting by Hans Jordaens III, KHM 38 (**left**) from the manuscript

catalogue of the collection of Manfredo Settala, Biblioteca Ambrosiana, Milan 38–39 engraved frontispiece of *Museum Septalanium* (Tortosa, 1664), BL 40–41 engraved frontispiece of Levinus Vincent, *Wondertooneel de nature* (Amsterdam, 1706) 41 engraving from Levinus Vincent, *Wondertooneel de nature* (Amsterdam, 1706) 42 engravings from Frederik Ruysch, *Thesaurus anatomicus* (Amsterdam, 1701) 43 (**top**) woodcut from Charles de Lecluse, *Exoticorum Libri decem* (Leyden, 1605) 43 (**bottom**) woodcut from Conrad Gesner, *Thierbuch* (Zurich, 1563) 44–45 illustration of the Viennese Imperial Collection from Ferdinand Storffer, *Specification of those pictures…* (1730), KHM 46 Isidore Bardi, *Still Life with Exotic Birds*, c. 1800, Musée du Louvre, Paris 47 MS D'Orville 539, Bodleian Library, Oxford 48 painting by Georg Haintz, Kunsthalle, Hamburg 49 Musée des Beaux-Arts, Rennes. Photo: Bridgeman 50–51 shells from the manuscript catalogue of the collection of Fernando Cospi, University Library, Bologna 52 coin cabinet, SA. Photo: KHM 53 amber cabinet, GG 54–55 woodcuts from Ulisse Aldrovandi, *Monstrorum historia* (Bologna, 1642) 56–57 painting by Anton Mozart, Museum of Decorative Arts, Berlin 58 Kunstschranck (Augsburg, 1625), Paul Getty Museum, Los Angeles; assemblage on top of cabinet by Samiya Swoboda-Nichols, 2000, Edward Swoboda Collection, Beverly Hills. 59–62 details of the interior of the cabinet of Gustavus Adolphus. Photos: Massimo Listri 63 exterior of the cabinet of Gustavus Adolphus, Uppsala University Library 64 writing cabinet by Wenzel Jamnitzer, GG 68–69 shell drinking-cup, KHM 70–71 The Yarmouth Collection, Norwich Castle Museum. Photo: Bridgeman 72 mineral cabinet, FS. Photo: Klaus E. Göltz 73 figure by Balthasar Permoser (1651–1732), GG 73 (**bottom**) woodcut from *Aldrovandi Museum metallicum* (Bologna, 1648) 74 (**left**) stone cup, Medici Collection, Museo degli Argenti, Florence. Photo: Scala 74 (**right**) jade mask, Museo degli Argenti, Florence. Photo: Scala 74 (**background**) engraving from Basilius Besler, *Fasciculus rariorum varii generis* (Nuremberg, 1622) 75 Grotto of the Animals, Medici Villa, Castello. Photo: Scala 76 panel from the

Uppsala Cabinet. Photo: Massimo Listri 77 sunflower, Mueseo dell' Opificio delle Pietre Dure, Florence. Photo: Scala 78 detail from *Shells* by Bartolomeo Bimbi, Palazzo delle Provincia, Siena 78 (**background**) engraving from Basilius Besler, *Fasciculus rariorum varii generis* (Nuremberg, 1622) 79 detail from A. Allori, *Pearl Fishers*. Photo: Scala 80 double nautilus shell, Museo degli Argenti. Photo: Massimo Listri 81 nautilus shell drinking-cup, GG 82/87 manuscript catalogue of Cospi Collection by G. Tosi, Bologna University Library. Photo: Massimo Listri 83–86 Arcimboldesque figures, Tuscany, early seventeenth century. Museo degli Argenti, Florence. Photos: Massimo Listri 87–88 coral display, North Gallery, SA. Photo: KHM 89 (**top**) ostrich egg with coral ornament, SA 89 (**bottom right**) coral amulet, Schatzkammer des Residenzmuseum, Munich 90 engraving from Levinus Vincent, *Wondertooneel de nature*, (Amsterdam, 1706) 91 drinking-cups, GG 92 *Daphne*, GG 93 detail of coral grotto, probably Genoa, SA. Photo: KHM 94 Frederik II of Gotha, c. 1700. Friedenstein Castle, Gotha. Photo: Massimo Listri 95 the wax cabinet, FS. Photo: Klaus E. Göltz 96–97 wax portraits from the Danish Royal Collections, Rosenborg Castle, Copenhagen 98–99 crocodile sand container, courtesy of Busch Reisinger Museum, Harvard University, Mass. (Gift of Stanley Marcus) 98–99 (**background**) engravings from Basilius Besler, *Fasciculus rariorum varii generis* (Nuremberg, 1622) 100–101 'Schüttelkästchen', SA. Photo: KHM 102 detail of ewer by Wenzel Jamnitzer, Schatzkammer des Residenzmuseum, Munich 103 cast of an eagle's claw supporting nautilus cup, South German, 1580, BM 103 (**bottom**) box for writing set, Wenzel Jamnitzer, c. 1570, SA. Photo: KHM 104–105 engraving from Levinus Vincent, *Wondertooneel de nature* (Amsterdam, 1706) 104 (**insets**) Anatomical Museum, University of Leyden 105 crocodile embryo, FS. Photo: Klaus E. Göltz 106–107 engravings from Frederik Ruysch, *Thesaurus anatomicus* (Amsterdam, 1701), BL 106 bronze dragon, Victoria & Albert Museum, London 106 (**bottom**) mermaid, Museo Civico Archeologico, Modena 108 'Todlein schrein', SA. Photo: KHM

109 Death as hunter, SA. Photo: KHM
110 engraving from Frederik Ruysch, *Thesaurus anatomicus* (Amsterdam, 1701), BL 111 engravings from Fortunius Liceti, *De monstrorum Libri, decem* 111 (**right**) woodcut from Ulisse Aldrovandi, *Monstrorum historia* (Bologna, 1642) 112 engraving from Fortunius Liceti, *De monstrorum Libri, decem* 112–113 Bartlolmeo Bimbi, *Two-headed lamb*, Palazzo Pitti. Photo: Massimo Listri 114 engravings from Basilius Besler, *Fasciculus rariorum varii generis* (Nuremberg, 1622) 114 (**background**) woodcut from Ulisse Aldrovandi, *Monstrorum historia* (Bologna, 1642) 115 woodcut from Conrad Gesner, *Thierbuch* (Zurich, 1563) 116 automata, Victoria & Albert Museum, London 117 devil automata, Civiche Raccolte d'Arte Applicata, Castello Sforzesco, Milan 118 clock automata by Melchior Maier, KHM 119 musical gondola, SA 120 astronomical clock, from the Gottorf Collection, Rosenborg Castle, Copenhagen 121 astronomical clock with armillary sphere, from Gottorf Collection, Rosenborg Castle, Copenhagen. Photo: John Lee, NM Copenhagen 122 engraving from Wenzel Jamnitzer, *Perspectiva Corporum Regularium* (Nuremberg, 1568) 122 ivory tower, Museo degli Argenti, Florence 123 ivory towers, GG 124–125 South German cabinet. Museum of Decorative Arts, Cologne 124–125 (**background**) engravings from Wenzel Jamnitzer, *Perspectiva Corporum Regularium* (Nuremberg, 1568) 126–127 woodcuts from Lorenz Stoer, *Geometria et perspectica* (Augsburg, 1576) 128–129 Giuseppe Arcimboldo, *Rudolf II as Vertumnus*, Skokloster, Sweden. Photo: Bridgeman 130–131 engraving by M. Merian the Elder. Photo: AKG 130 portrait of Archduke Ferdinand II (1529–95), SA 131 portrait of Philippa Welser, wife of Archduke Ferdinand II, married 1554, SA 132 Naturalia Gallery, SA. Photo: KHM 133 the Spanish Room, SA. Photo: AKG 134 musical instrument, SA 135 Christopher Gardner, Tirolean grotesque figure, end sixteenth century, SA. Photo: KHM 136–137 anonymous painting of a cripple, SA. Photo: KHM 138 anonymous painting, SA 139 anonymous painting, SA 140–141 E. de Critz, *John Tradescant and Roger Friend*, Ashmolean Museum, Oxford 142 Riley, *Elias Ashmole*, Ashmolean Museum, Oxford. Photo: Bridgeman

143 attributed to Cornelius de Neve, *John Tradescant the Elder*, Ashmolean Museum, Oxford. Photo: Bridgeman 144–145 Claude du Molinet, engravings from *Le Cabinet de la Bibliothèque Ste-Geneviève* (Paris, 1692) 146–147 portrait and engravings from *Museo Cospiano* (Bologna, 1677), BL 148–149 illustrations from the Aldrovandi Codex, University Library, Bologna 148 woodcut from Aldrovandi, *Monstrorum historia* (Bologna, 1642) 150 engraving of Ulisse Aldrovandi at the age of 78 151 engravings from *Museo Cospiano* (Bologna, 1677) 152–153 engravings from the Aldrovandi Codex, Bologna University Library 155 ivory tower, Museo degli Argenti, Florence 156 composite heads from the Settala Collection, Biblioteca Ambrosiana, Milan 157 portrait of Manfredo Settala, Biblioteca Ambrosiana, Milan 158–159 drawings from the Settala Collection catalogue, Biblioteca Ambrosiana, Milan 160 portrait and frontispiece engraving from *Museum Kircherianum* (Milan, Rome, 1763) 161 engravings from *Physiologia Kircheriana* (Amsterdam, 1680) and *Musurgia universalis* (Rome, 1650) 162–163 engravings from *Physiologia Kircheriana* (Amsterdam, 1680) and *Musurgia universalis* (Rome, 1650) 164 wax portrait by Wenzel Maller, 1606, Victoria and Albert Museum, London 165 illustration from the museum catalogue of Rudolf II's collection, 1621, Österreichische Nationalbibliothek, Vienna 165 (**bottom**) engraving from Georg Hoefnagel, *Archetype* (Frankfurt, 1592) 166–167 engravings from Georg Hoefnagel, *Archetype* (Frankfurt, 1592) 168 Gasparo Miseroni, handle of tazza, KHM 169 Gasparo Miseroni, detail lapis lazuli tazza, KHM 170 clock by Hans Schotteim, Augsburg, 1580, BM 171 engraving from L.E. Bergeron, *Manuel du turneur* (Paris, 1792) 172 cup of Nicholas Pfaff, 1611, KHM 173 detail from silver ewer by N. Schmidt, late sixteenth century, KHM 173 (**right**) Bezoar cup by Jan Vermeyen, *c*. 1600, KHM 174 portrait of the Elector Augustus the Pious, Gemäldegalerie, Dresden. Photo: Deutsche Fotothek 175 carved cherrystone in gold setting, GG 176–177 clockwork globes by Elias Lenker, Augsburg, 1629, GG 178 ivory oliphant, Sicily, *c*. 1100, GG 179 woodcut from Michael Herr's bestiary

(Strasbourg, 1546) 180 owl by Gottfried Döring, GG 181 goblet in the shape of a black girl, 1709, and dragon made of misshapen pearl, before 1706, GG 184–185 Jacques de Lajoue, *The Cabinet of Bonnier de la Mosson* (1739), Private Collection 186–187 engraving after Lajoue, *La Pharmacie*, Bibliothèque Nationale, Paris 188–189 J. B. Cortonne, *Designs for the cabinet of Bonnier de la Mosson* (1739), Bibliothèque d'Art et Archéologie, J. Doucet, Paris 190 engraving from the catalogue of E. F. Gersaint, 1736, BL 191 François Boucher, trade card of Gersaint, 1740, Bibliothèque Nationale, Paris 192 engraving of the shop of Remy, Bibliothèque Nationale, Paris 193 Mr Green's Museum, woodcut from the *Gentleman's Magazine*, 1788, London 195 'The Cabinet at Strawberry Hill' from *A Description of the Villa* (1784), Strawberry Hill, London 196 reliquary, Musée du Chateauroux 197 inkstand, Goodrich Court 198 watercolour by J. H. Gandy, Soane Museum. Photo: Bridgeman 199 drawing by Benjamin Zix, Musée du Louvre, Paris. Photo: RMN (by Jean Schormans) 200–201 engravings from S.R. Meyrick, *Ancient Arms and Armour from the Collection of Goodrich Court* (London, 1830) 202–203 watercolour after Sarah Stone (1760–1844), BM, Department of Ethnography Library 204–205 engraving of the studio of J. P. Dantan, Musée Carnavalet, Paris, Photothèque des musées de la ville de Paris 206 'The Leverian Museum' from *Companion to the Museum of Sir Ashton Lever* (1790), London 207 Charles Willson Peale's Museum, Pensylvania Academy of Fine Arts, Philadelphia 208 engravings from S. R. Meyrick, *Ancient Arms and Armour from the Collection of Goodrich Court* (1830), London 210–211 collection of Alistair McAlpine. Photo: Graham Harrison, *The World of Interiors* 215 Photo: Giselle Freund Anna Beskow Agency 217 photograph by Man Ray ©Man Ray Trust/ADAGP, Paris and DACS, London 2002 218 André Breton, *Pan hoplie*, 1953 © ADAGP, Paris and DACS, London 2002, collection of Eliza Breton, Paris 219 André Breton, *Poeme-objet*, 1941 © ADAGP, Paris and DACS, London 2002, Pierre Matisse Gallery Corp., New York 220 The work of J. C. Moreux 221 (**right top and bottom**) photo by Jean-Marie Del Moral

222 Victor Brauner, *Wolf table* © ADAGP, Paris and DACS, London 2002, Centre Pompidou, Paris. Photo: RMN (by Jacqueline Hyde) 223 Max Ernst, title-page of the *Journal d'un austronaute millenaire* (Paris, 1969) © ADAGP, Paric and DACS, London 2002 225 Joseph Cornell and Bill Jacobson, *Museum*, 1944–48 © The Joseph and Robert Cornell Memorial Foundation/VAGA, New York/DACS, London 2002. Photo: The Joseph and Robert Cornell Memorial Foundation 226 Joseph Cornell, *Pharmacy*, 1943 © The Joseph and Robert Cornell Memorial Foundation/VAGA, New York/DACS, London 2002, Private Collection 227 Joseph Cornell, *Hotel Eden*, *c*. 1945 © The Joseph and Robert Cornell Memorial Foundation/VAGA, New York/DACS, London 2002, National Gallery of Canada, Ottawa 228 Guillaume Bijl, *The Cabinet of Claude Gouffier* © DACS 2002, Château d'Oiron. Photo: Laurent Lecat 229 Christian Boltanski, *Portrait Gallery* © ADAGP, Paris and DACS, London 2002, Château d'Oiron. Photo: Laurent Lecat 230 Thomas Grünfeld, *Misfit* © DACS 2002, Château d'Oiron. Photo: Laurent Lecat 231 Thomas Grünfeld, *Pegasus* © DACS 2002, Château d'Oiron. Photo: Laurent Lecat 232 Mario Merz, *Niger Crocodile*, 1972 Musée National d'Art Moderne, Centre Georges Pompidou, Paris 233 Natasha Nicholson, *Cabinet of Curiosities*, 2000, by permission of the artist 234 Mark Dion and Robert Williams, *Theatrum Mundi*, 2001. Photos: Roger Lee 237 Claude Lalanne, *Flies* © ADAGP, Paris and DACS, London 2002. Photo: Jean-Marie Del Moral 238–239 the studio of Miquel Barceló. Photo: Jean-Marie Del Moral 240–243 the collection of Françoise de Nobèle. Photo: Jean-Marie Dell Moral 244–247 the apartment of Solange Fouilleul. Photo: Jean-Marie Del Moral 248–249 the collections of Alistair McAlpine, Photos: Graham Harrison, *The World of Interiors* 252 engraving of Mary Davis from Ormerund, *History of the County Palatine and the City of Chester* (1676)

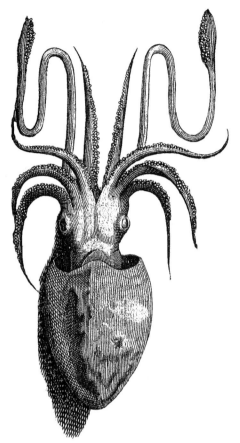

Acknowledgments

For their help in the drafting of certain passages and the compilation of the notes and bibliography, the author wishes to thank Bénédicte Savoy, Nicolas Carpentiers, Marc Chevalier, Lionel Leforestier and Ian Sutton.

I am also grateful to the following, without whom this work would not have come to fruition: Miquel Barceló, Françoise de Nobèle, Solange Fouilleul, Denise Jacquelin, Isabelle Jammes, François-Xavier Lalanne, France Le Queffelec and Jean-Marie Del Moral who specially photographed certain places and *objets de curiosité* in Paris collections.

Endpapers: Erik Desmazières (b. 1948) has worked on the theme of eccentric architecture associated with learning (libraries and studios). As part of a series relating to Jorge Luis Borges' 'Library of Babel' he produced this etching of a cabinet of curiosities for a catalogue of the Librairie Jammes in Paris in 1998.

Index